CONTENTS

PREFACE

by Harry Dalton, General Manager

In the last quarter century, as major league baseball has expanded and the demand for big league players has increased, more and more organizations have put greater emphasis on player development, adding coaches to their minor league staffs, joining special instructional leagues that operate in the fall, and giving standardized instruction to all players in the organization, no matter at what level.

The organizational instruction manual is a natural result of the increased stress on player development. Until the 1950s few, if any, major league organizations printed instructional manuals. Many big league organizations have them today, and in many cases they are similar. As instructional personnel changed clubs they brought their own particular styles of teaching with them, with the result that many organizations today have instructional programs that reflect the contributions of many qualified baseball men. The *Major League Baseball Manual* is such a product. A portion of the basis for this manual comes from work done in the late 1950s at the Baltimore Orioles' minor league training camp in Thomasville, Georgia. Additions and revisions, of course, have come from all directions, and on the pages ahead you will find the result of the current Brewers' instructional staff, headed by Scouting and Development Director, Ray Poitevint.

The theory behind our manual is simple—teach young players from their first day in the Brewer organization the way we want them to execute baseball fundamentals and repeat that instruction throughout their professional careers right through their stay with the Brewers. The style of play printed here is not the only way to play baseball—but it is the Brewers' way. It is our hope that the information on the pages ahead will help many of you improve your play, whether amateur or professional, and help even more of you enjoy and appreciate more easily the performance of others as you watch our great game.

TO ALL MANAGERS

So that each manager and all players throughout the Milwaukee Brewers' minor league system will have a better understanding of fundamentals, and so that a standardized set of instructions can be used as a guide, we have set forth, with the help of many qualified teachers in our organization, a plan that we feel will be helpful not only to the players but to the managers as well. In reviewing this manual, please look upon it as one method of making yourself and players much better qualified persons in your chosen professions.

The manual stresses the importance of basic fundamentals and should be used at all levels. With an emphasis on preparing the young player for the major league club as rapidly as possible, make certain that the development and instructional programs are not only carried out during the spring training season but during the championship season as well.

PREPARE YOURSELVES PHYSICALLY AND MENTALLY TO *DO A JOB*.

THE MANAGER'S RESPONSIBILITY

The successful operation of a baseball club at any level requires the closest cooperation between manager, business manager, and player. Although each has his own well-defined sphere of responsibility and neither should attempt in any way to exceed it or to intrude upon the duties of the other, all must work together toward a mutual understanding which will create harmony—and this is essential for success.

The manager, general manager, and player should each make certain that all equipment and other facilities are taken care of to the utmost. Players and managers should be neat and make every effort in establishing a clean dressing room and clean uniforms, and in surrounding themselves with a pleasant atmosphere. This can be done by taking a little time and making extra efforts in your clubhouse, both at home and on the road. Have pride when wearing your uniform and have pride in seeing that your surroundings are well kept.

It is the direct responsibility of the managers to see that all players on minor league clubs in the Milwaukee organization wear some type of protective helmet or insert in both games and batting practice. The manager should see that this is done at all times.

HANDLING PLAYERS OFF FIELD

PLAYERS MUST CONDUCT THEMSELVES AS GENTLEMEN AT ALL TIMES. SEE TO IT THAT THERE IS:

No gambling at any time.

No profane language.

No roughhousing in hotels.

No yelling back at fans.

No unkind remarks to women at any time.

No excessive staying in bed in the morning.

No excessive drinking of any kind.

No eating of junk foods—proper diet is essential.

PROPER DRESS IS IMPORTANT FOR A PROFESSIONAL ATHLETE. MAKE CERTAIN THE PLAYER:

Is neat and well-groomed in the hotels as well as in the home city of his club. Shoes should be worn at all times. Sandals are permissible, but stockings should be worn with them. Hair and sideburns should be trimmed. Extra-long hair will not be allowed.

WHEN A PLAYER IS BEING SENT FROM ONE CLUB TO ANOTHER, NEVER SEND PLAYER AWAY WITHOUT:

1. Talking to him in private office.
2. Telling him of weaknesses he may have to work on.
3. Stressing the importance of reporting to the assigned club immediately.
4. Advising him to tell the new manager if he has any type of injury that may hamper his playing ability.
5. Giving him your sealed written report to deliver to his next manager, detailing what special work the player needs and how you feel player should be handled.

HANDLING PLAYERS ON FIELD

MANAGERS:

We have committed ourselves to development . . . let's develop.

Emphasize the importance of fundamentals.

Be the best baseball teacher in the baseball world.

Knowledge will overcome fear and indecision.

Prepare yourselves to give the player this knowledge.

It is important to school the player correctly during the spring-training period.

It is equally important to continue this schooling throughout the season as well.

Organize your time.

Make sure every time you do something you do it for a purpose.

Every minute counts—use it correctly.

You are a leader . . . act like one.

Be aggressive and enthusiastic.

Instill confidence in the player.

Morning workouts are important for players' development.

Emphasize the importance of speed and stealing bases.

Create a desire within the player to win.

Both players and managers should be organized.

Don't waste time once you get on the field.

Meetings should take place in clubhouse. Verbal discussions are important. Communicate.

Never show up player. Discuss his mistakes privately.

Other teams hope to win. We expect to win.

MANAGERS SHOULD NEVER ALLOW:

Beer in the clubhouse for minors.

Horseplay by players in the bull pen and on the bench.

Lying around outside dugout or bull pen.

Players being late for meetings, bus, batting practice, etc.

Eating food or drinking soft drinks in the concession area. (Should the player have time to eat or drink, make certain he is in the clubhouse.)

A pitcher to try talking the manager into leaving him in the game.

CONDITIONING

It is generally conceded that strength is the most important single element in an athletic performance. In most sports, when we place one man against another, the stronger one has a marked advantage. This is especially true in the game of baseball. If two boys have the same degree of skill in playing baseball, the stronger individual has a much better chance to succeed. We have concluded that not only is there a very high correlation between strength and success in hitting and throwing a baseball, but there is also a definite improvement in the ability of the individual when his strength is noticeably increased.

What is the best way to acquire this strength? Many theories have been advanced. Ty Cobb ran in weighted shoes. Johnny Mize spent the winter chopping wood. Ted Williams did calisthenics. Many players have used weighted bats. Some have used weights. In each of those methods the physiological effect is similar. The muscle must work against resistance in order to increase in strength—it must be overloaded.

Swinging a weighted bat will certainly overload a muscle, but the weight of the bat must be increased gradually for strength to be increased. The same principle applies to chopping wood, running in weighted shoes, squeezing rubber balls, etc. The amount of the resistance must be increased to the point where the muscle is completely overloaded for maximum gain in strength.

The best way found to ease the load or the resistance to a muscle group is through a controlled weight-training program. If a boy will better himself by gaining strength, why not use weights? The load on the muscles can be increased gradually and a record of the progress can then be kept accurately. The number of repetitions or the duration of the overload effort can be controlled.

A baseball player must maintain a great deal of strength and endurance to play baseball over a long summer season. A well-conditioned cardiovascular system (heart, lungs) is necessary to maintain energy levels at their peak. Without proper endurance conditioning, a player is more likely to sustain injuries because muscles, ligaments, and tendons are not adequately supplied with oxygen and nutrients transported in the blood system.

Athletic teams that have established aerobic (endurance) type programs have reported improved performance and fewer injuries. Teams such as Brazilian soccer teams, the Green Bay Packers, the Dallas Cowboys, and Nebraska football teams have benefited from Heart/Lung Endurance Training. A professional athlete whose cardiovascular condition is at a high level is more alert, has improved concentration, and does not fatigue as fast as a non-conditioned athlete.

According to guidelines established by the American College of Sports Medicine (July 1978), without maintenance, cardiovascular (endurance) condition can deteriorate 50 percent in 4–12 weeks. Baseball game situations do not provide enough aerobic training. Late summer fatigue and decline in performance, which some players experience, could be reduced or eliminated with better endurance training.

Pitchers who maintain their running at high levels throughout the season seem to experience less arm fatigue and soreness (i.e., more efficient heart/lung system and large muscle groups, and better blood supply of oxygen to arms and areas that are being placed under great stress). In July and August, when many professional baseball teams reduce pitcher running schedules, it may be advisable to increase conditioning programs for a 3–4 week period so players have endurance for stretch runs.

When position players run with pitchers one or two days a week for 20–30 minutes it also provides cardiovascular benefits. However, low-intensity jogging for 20-minute periods may be a better alternative to prevent leg fatigue. Sprint running should be done on a daily basis in order not to lose over-all quickness.

For a player with low-back or leg problems, swimming can be used for a conditioning program. If a heart rate is maintained between 120–160 this should not cause fatigue. The traditional crawl stroke need not be used. A kicking exercise, walking, running, or bouncing across the pool, or a breast or side stroke may be beneficial.

During games, range of motion exercises are important between innings to keep joints lubricated and muscles stretched. Even more attention needs to be given to flexibility in cold weather.

LOOSENING UP

All players should realize how important their legs are to them as professional baseball players. Healthy legs can mean the difference between success and failure as an athlete.

We want all Milwaukee Brewers' players to be conditioned so they will stay free from injury. As a precautionary measure, all players, both regular and extra men, must loosen up their legs when first going on the ball field. This will be done before any catch is played or any pepper games started. The player will be required to do this by running on the sidelines or by going completely around the park.

It is part of your duties to see that this is done each day. Pitchers, of course, will run as directed by you.

Stretching exercises are to be done together and supervised by your trainer.

MORNING WORKOUT REPORT

Morning workouts should be held often, and the following report form should be completed and sent to the Milwaukee office.

TEAM: DATE:

MANAGER: LENGTH OF WORKOUT:

PLAYERS INVOLVED:

WEAKNESSES OF PLAYERS:

PROGRESS:

BATTING PRACTICE

THE FOLLOWING BATTING PRACTICE PROCEDURE IS TO BE USED AT ALL TIMES.

BATTING PRACTICE ROUTINE:

2 Bunts
2 Hit and Runs
1 Squeeze
5 Swings

1. Upon completion of swings the hitter becomes a runner at 1B.

2. He runs to 2B on first hit-and-run attempt (remembering to glance back at the hitter and pick up the ball).

3. He runs to 3B on second hit-and-run attempt (once again glancing in at hitter to pick up the ball).

4. Runner then breaks from 3B as pitcher's arm comes forward and hitter executes suicide squeeze bunt.

5. On-deck hitter fields all bunts.

6. Pitchers—if you wish to work on breaking balls while throwing BP, then throw them on the hit-and-run attempts to each hitter, thus enabling the hitter to work on going the other way with the breaking ball in a running situation.

7. Any extra time for batting practice can be used for base-hit rounds with all position players at the cage and the pitchers shagging.

8. On occasion try making base-hit rounds competitive by having the infielders compete against the outfielders.

PRE-GAME DRILLS

OUTFIELDERS

LF	Two throws to 2B	Three throws home
CF	Two throws to 3B	Three throws home
RF	Two throws to 3B	Three throws home

On all balls hit to OF, make sure outfielder is given opportunity to charge ground balls and also make him move. Don't make fly balls routine—move him around.

INFIELDERS

Round	Direction of Ball	Speed of Ball	Play Procedure
1	Directly to player	Normal	Throw to 1B—get one
2	Feather toward 2B	Normal	Throw to 1B—get one
3	Feather toward foul line	Normal	Throw to 1B—get one
4	Feather toward 2B	Hard	Throw to 2B—get two
5	Feather toward foul line	Hard	Throw to 2B—get two
6	Directly to player	Easy	a. Throw to 1B—get one b. First baseman throw to 3B
7	Directly to player	Normal	Throw home for tag
8	Pop fly to catcher		

THE FINAL WORD

Cooperate to the utmost with the local club. Make certain that public appearances are made by you and your team members. Be a hustling-type team that the city and the Brewers can be proud of. Do everything you possibly can to assist in bringing fans to the ball park. Your players should sign autographs. When they cannot, they should be polite. They should never ignore and brush past fans.

Remember, however, that you are a member of the Milwaukee Brewers' organization and you are employed by them. In spite of the understandable pressure put on you by local representatives to win, win, please do not lose sight of what your responsibilities are.

No one wants to win more than you do—nor more than this organization does. Bear in mind that you have the extremely important task of handling our greatest assets—the major league stars of the future. We have entrusted the young player to you, and it is your responsibility to safeguard his future and never allow anything, not even the winning of a ball game, to take away from his development or bring about an injury.

TO THE FINEST
PROFESSIONAL
ATHLETES
IN THE WORLD

On the following pages we have compiled basic fundamentals and instrumental guides that you should use in preparing yourself for your major league career.

These fundamentals and instructions should be used at all levels of development, and they are set forth so that the Milwaukee Brewers' system of development gives the player the same pattern to follow throughout his career as a Brewer player.

We have touched on all positions and have prepared outlines for both offensive and defensive baseball.

I would like to acknowledge all Brewers' instructors and particularly the following for their contributions:

George Bamberger	—	Pitching
Sam Suplizio	—	Outfield play and baserunning
Tom Gamboa	—	Hitting
Lee Sigman	—	Infield play
Jerry Weinstein	—	Catching
Johnny Neun	—	First base

Their help is greatly appreciated in preparing this Manual.

PREPARE YOURSELVES PHYSICALLY AND MENTALLY TO *DO A JOB!*

Ray R. Poitevint
*Director of Player
Procurement*

24

PITCHING

SPRING TRAINING

SOFT TOSS: Beginning from day #1, pitchers are to stretch out long distance using fast ball and change-up; the final 5 minutes are always to be spent on breaking balls. Soft toss should start at 60 feet and progress to a distance of 150 feet for at least 15 minutes each day. This is to develop all the muscles a pitcher uses in his assortment of pitches.

WORKOUTS: Workouts are to be tailored as much as possible to needs of the individual, especially players coming off arm problems or other physical ailments.

Group #1 (little or no previous throwing prior to spring training)

Begin with 5–10 minutes on the side and increase work load daily. Should be able to throw 15–20 minutes of batting practice after 5 days, and pitch in games in 9 or 10 days.

Group #2 (primarily West Coast players coming out of winter league)

Begin with 15–20 minutes batting practice; ready for intra-squad games in approximately 6 days.

SPRING-TRAINING CONDITIONING:

1. All pitchers to participate in preliminary sprints, stretching, calisthenics, long toss, and endurance running.
2. At the end of each day, pitchers will run together in the following pattern—

DAY	SPRINTS	DISTANCE
1	10	75 yards
2	12	"
3	14	"
4	16	"
5	18	"
6	20	"
7	20	"

EXAMPLE OF DAILY RUNNING:

Sprint ——————— jog ——————— walk ——————— sprint (repeat 20 times)

50 pickups

Warm Down ——— 3–6 minutes jogging; 5–10 minutes of stretching.

Recuperation by one or all of the following—walking, jogging, standing still. After 20 repetitions are reached, the *rest interval* time will be *decreased*. Pickups will go from 25–50. The warm down includes jogging and stretching.

GENERAL COMMENTS:

1. All pitchers will change sweatshirts after throwing unless they move directly into running.
2. All pitchers to run together as much as possible.
3. Pitchers requesting extra work are to finish up in bull pen.

SPRING-TRAINING LECTURE SESSIONS:

1. Cover pitcher's responsibilities regarding defense of bunts, position on field after base hits or other batted balls.
2. Review balk rules.
3. Measure objectively, with examination, material covered.
4. Review cutoff assignments.

PITCHING

THE GREATEST ASSET A PITCHER CAN HAVE IS COMMAND: COMMAND OF HIMSELF AND COMMAND OF HIS PITCHES.

TO BE A CONSISTENT WINNER, A PITCHER MUST:

1.   Have good control. Get first pitch over for a strike.

2.   Know how to field his position.

3.   Analyze the hitters—strengths and weaknesses.

4.   Have confidence.

5.   Keep his body active, especially the legs.

6.   Form good pitching habits.

7.   Concentrate—pick out a spot and throw to it.

8.   Communicate with his catcher—understand each other.

9.   Pitch a ball game. Don't just be a thrower.

10.   Back up all bases.

11.   Be sure to cover 1B.

12.   THINK.

GETTING THE SIGNS:

1.   Take signs on rubber and be relaxed.

2.   Don't always accept first sign.

3.   Use head and glove for deception.

PITCHER SHOULD LEAD WITH HIS ELBOW.

PITCHING

4. Shake catcher off.

5. Pump once, twice, three times. Don't form a pattern so that hitter can time you. Do something different. Walk around mound. Make hitter wait.

6. After sign and when going into delivery, use glove and body to hide ball.

POSITION ON RUBBER:

1. Right-hand pitcher pitches from right corner of rubber.

2. Left-hand pitcher pitches from left corner of rubber. This is done to allow pitcher to deliver ball from behind hitter (a more effective angle).

3. When right-hand pitcher faces left-hand hitter he may want to move a little more toward the center but not directly in the center because this will cut down on angle. Left-hander may do the same thing when throwing to right-hand hitter.

PITCHERS MUST:

1. Try and stay ahead of hitter.

2. Have hitter hit pitcher's pitch.

3. Know best pitch on given night and use this when in trouble.

4. Have confidence.

5. Know own weaknesses and try to correct them.

6. Know the outs, score.

7. Know the importance of the outs and the runners on base (tying and winning).

8. Know who is covering base.

9. Know the speed of his own infielders.

10. Never show temper and fight umpires. They could get even.

11. Keep control of yourself when errors are made behind you. If you can't control yourself, you can't control the ball.

12. Pick up target before making pitch.

13. Be the boss when you are on the mound. BE MEAN AND AG-GRESSIVE. Don't let the hitter take the money out of your pocket.

SOME HELPFUL SUGGESTIONS TO MAKE SUCCESSFUL PITCHERS:

The minor league Pitching Coach is there to help. He will determine delivery changes and help correct overstriding. Decide whether a pitcher is better at three quarter or over the top. Use him and his knowledge.

A manager should give each pitcher the opportunity to start at different times during the regular season. No one should be kept strictly in the relief role. Stay with a starting rotation, then deviate from time to time without throwing a staff into a complete change. Some new competent starter may be found.

SOME PHYSICAL ADJUSTMENTS FOR MANAGERS TO CONSIDER:

1. Watch your pitcher's elbow. See that he leads with this. Keep it parallel to the ground, or higher, so as to force him to stay on top of the ball.

2. Watch your pitcher to see that he has cocked wrist.

3. Wrist can be cocked by making sure wrist is down.

4. Straight change should be taught all pitchers. Easy way of learning it is throwing with three fingers and pushing ball as far back in hand as possible. Better control, etc.

5. Experiment and change grip and delivery for better life on fastball.

6. Pitchers should hold men on with hands resting on belt buckle or in vicinity of belt buckle. Hands and arms should be relaxed.

MAKE SURE WRIST IS COCKED.

PROPER GRIP FOR A CURVEBALL.

PROPER GRIP FOR A FORKBALL.

PROPER GRIP FOR A KNUCKLEBALL.

PROPER GRIP FOR A FASTBALL.

7. Pitchers having curveball trouble should throw to hitter having trouble hitting curveball. This can be done in a batting cage or during batting practice.

8. Squeeze rubber ball to strengthen fingers and hand.

9. If pitcher is wild high consistently, he should pick up new target. Throw to top of shoes, left knee, right knee. Forget about center of glove. Think low and pitch low.

10. Pitchers who fail to shove hard enough off back leg and get no push should be advised and instructed that bringing up front leg higher will automatically put extra pressure on back leg and cause pitcher to get shove he needs. This also will aid deception since pitcher can then hide glove behind front leg as he brings it up.

11. When you push, PUSH HARD AND TOWARD HOME PLATE.

12. Pitchers who have habit of wearing cap back on head can sometimes improve control by pulling cap down. This may help block out distractions by narrowing pitcher's area of concentration.

FOR A BETTER CURVEBALL:

1. Put pressure on the middle finger.

2. Put pressure on the thumb.

3. Use the index finger as a guide.

4. Keep elbow up parallel with shoulder.

5. Cock wrist.

6. Pull down hard, like pulling down shade.

7. Follow through.

8. Bring hand and arm into opposite side of throwing arm.

9. To force arm to follow through, slap self in back.

10. Snap wrist.

11. Warm up slowly with breaking ball to get proper spin.

12. Stay on top.

FOR A BETTER CHANGE-UP:

1. Main purpose is to upset batter's timing.

2. Can be thrown by using 2, 3, or 4 fingers and the thumb to grip ball.

3. Keep tips of fingers off of ball. Place in rear of palm.

4. Drag your back (push-off) foot.

5. Good change must have appearance of fastball.

6. Don't be afraid of throwing change-up too hard. Biggest mistake is when pitcher lets up on delivery.

FIELDING

FIELDING POSITION:

1. When you release the ball you are no longer pitcher but now another infielder and should be alert and ready to make all plays.

2. All balls hit to the left of the pitcher, immediately break for 1B. If necessary, cover 1B. If not, keep out of play. The pitcher should take all possible bunts. Listen to the catcher to determine what base to throw to.

3. Make certain when play is to be made at either 3B or home plate that you run halfway between the two bases and then determine what base you must back up as runners advance and throw comes in.

FIELDING BUNTS:

1. Break hard going in. (Shove off back leg and bounce off mound.)

2. Make sure you see ball go into glove before looking at target.

3. Depending upon chosen defense with man on 1B and 2B and bunt in order, (a) pitcher covers 3B side and third baseman stays back, (b) pitcher covers 1B side and first baseman stays back. (This is explained in detail on pages 184, 186.)

FIELDING BALLS BUNTED DOWN FIRST-BASE LINE AND THROWING TO FIRST BASE:

1. Right-hand pitcher doesn't have time to straighten up. Will stay down low and throw inside diamond so that first baseman gets a good picture of the ball. May even have to throw underhanded depending upon time involved and closeness to the bag.

2. Left-hand pitcher must pivot to his right and do a half turn. Be sure to have something on the throw and keep inside of diamond so that the throw will not hit runner in the back.

FIELDING BALL BUNTED STRAIGHT AT PITCHER AND THROWING TO FIRST BASE:

1. Take a short crow hop. Set yourself and throw with something on it.

FIELDING BALL BUNTED DOWN THIRD-BASE LINE AND THROWING TO FIRST BASE:

1. Right-hand pitcher goes to right side, plants his right foot and comes up throwing.

2. Left-hand pitcher fields ball in glove, pivots to his right on a half turn, and comes up throwing in two counts.

FIELDING BUNTS AND THROWING TO SECOND BASE:

1. Know who is covering and listen for catcher to call play.

2. Make sure body is controlled. Don't throw off balance.

3. Right-hand pitcher on ball bunted to his left will field ball, plant right foot and make a half pivot, open up hip, and throw with something on it.

4. Right-hand pitcher with ball bunted to his right will field ball, do a complete pivot to his left throwing off right leg, and have something on throw.

5. Left-hand pitcher with ball bunted to his left will field ball, do a half pivot planting left foot, and then throw with something on it— all in one motion.

6. Left-hand pitcher with ball bunted to his right will field ball, plant left leg, open up on pivot to right—depending upon where ball is fielded—and throw to 2B with something on it.

PITCHING

FIELDING BUNTS AND THROWING TO THIRD BASE:

1. Right-hand pitcher when fielding ball to his right fields ball and does a pivot to his left opening hips, planting back foot, and throwing to 3B (a complete turn most times necessary).

2. Right-hand pitcher when fielding ball to his left does a complete turn, plants back leg, and throws in a hurry (a difficult play).

3. Left-hand pitcher on ball to his left charges line, fields ball, does half pivot, plants foot, and throws.

4. Left-hand pitcher on ball to his right fields ball, stays down low, opens up hips, and throws sidearm or gives underhand shove to 3B, depending upon where ball is fielded.

COVERING FIRST BASE:

1. Break hard for bag. Take throw about 5 feet from bag—staying inside and touching bag with whichever foot comes up.

2. After tagging bag, turn in toward diamond so that runner won't step or run into you.

3. Should there be men on the other bases, turning in also prepares you for a throw to third or possibly home. Be alert.

4. Pitcher should not snatch at ball. Don't fight it. Be relaxed when fielding this tossed ball.

5. When first baseman boots ground ball, go to the bag in the same fashion but when ball is kicked stay at bag. Do not run by. Put one foot on bag, then stretch out as would a first baseman.

THROWING TO SECOND BASE FOR DOUBLE PLAY:

1. Always know who is covering bag so you can lead correctly. Most times it will be shortstop since he is coming toward bag and it is easier for pitcher to throw to him and for him to execute the double play.

2. Pitcher should lead throw to shortstop.

3. Throw to second baseman should be thrown directly to the bag.

DOUBLE-HINGED SHIN GUARDS OFFER THE BEST PROTECTION IN THE BASIC CATCHING STANCE AND THE WIRE MASK FACILITATES THE VIEW OF THE LOW PITCH AND OF THE BALL IN THE DIRT.

CATCHING

BLOCKING THE BALL

Though pitching obviously is the dominant force in baseball, you have to remember that the man most responsible for the pitcher's performance is the catcher. An outstanding catcher can help make a good pitcher out of an ordinary one, while a mediocre catcher can impair the effectiveness of even a Moose Haas or a Mike Caldwell.

The catcher's chief contribution lies in his handling of the pitches, particularly the low pitch and the one in the dirt. Our pitchers live and die with the low pitch, and we'd rather see them pitch into the dirt than put the ball over waist high. They must have confidence in their ability to keep the ball down and in their catcher's ability to handle it.

Remember, whereas the improper handling of a normal pitch can cost the pitcher a strike and put him in a hole, the bungling of the pitch in the dirt could cost the game. It could result in a run, an advance of a base, the loss of a double-play situation, etc.

The handling of the ball in the dirt is, therefore, of vital importance and should be worked on every day.

The first imperative is top-flight gear. The catcher must be equipped with a protective cup, double-hinged shin guards, a protective helmet, and a wire mask.

We prefer the double-hinged shin guards because they offer better protection in the basic catching stance, and we prefer the wire mask because it facilitates the view of the low pitch and ball in the dirt.

The catcher's stance greatly affects his mobility and quickness. It must enable him to handle anything in and out of the strike zone as well as in the dirt.

FEET SHOULD BE WIDER THAN SHOULDERS.

A wide flat-footed stance with the feet wider than the shoulders and the hips set above the knees provides balance as well as mobility. Point: The actual alignment of the feet is not as important as the flat-footed effect with the weight up on the balls of the feet.

The catcher must make sure not to overbalance on one foot or the other so that the heel comes off the ground. That will shunt most of the weight to the foot so that the catcher will often be forced to shift his weight to the opposite foot before moving toward the ball.

The tendency to elevate the right heel compounds the problem of lateral mobility, since most wild pitches are thrown to the catcher's right. The loss of mobility to the left is not as critical, since the right-handed catcher has his glove on that side.

Most catchers attack the bouncing pitch too aggressively. They try to catch the ball rather than block it. We prefer a more passive approach. We want the catcher to block the ball so that it stays close to and in front of him.

CATCHING

HIPS SHOULD BE ABOVE KNEES.

We teach this with a technique called "walling the ball." The catcher goes to his knees (wide base) and places his hands, thumbs out, between his legs.

This prevents him from being struck on the elbow, causing injury or deflecting the flight of the ball.

In blocking the fastball in the dirt (right or left), the catcher must get his hips and outside shoulder around the ball, not just square off with it. The catcher must block the outside pitch by getting around to the outside of the ball and deadening the rebound.

To block the fastball over the middle, the catcher need only go to his knees and let the ball rebound off his chest and drop in front of him. He can keep the ball from running up his chest or over his head by letting his shoulders roll forward to cup the ball.

The best way to play one of those 55-foot fastballs is in soccer goalie fashion—blocking or snaring the ball as best you can.

BLOCK THE BALL, DON'T CATCH IT.

The curveball or slider into the dirt presents a different problem, as it rebounds in the direction opposite its spin. For example, the right-handed curve will bounce to the catcher's left, the distance depending upon the velocity and rotation of the pitch.

On a right-hand curveball to the catcher's right, therefore, the receiver should stay on the inside of the ball rather than round the ball with his hips. A good rule of thumb on this pitch is to play the ball off the right shoulder, allowing for the ball to back up.

The catcher can prepare for errant breaks by putting more weight on the foot away from the anticipated break. Since most breaking balls in the dirt break away from the catcher, this "onweighting" allows the catcher to shift.

The catcher can also gain an advantage by adjusting his stance. The slider is generally thrown to a specific half of the plate—in to a lefty and

CATCHING

"WALLING" THE BALL.

down and away from a righty (right-handed hitter). The catcher can gain a half step on any pitch that goes into the dirt by sliding inside or outside just before the pitch is delivered.

The same technique can be used on the curveball, depending on the type of curve, its velocity, and the pitcher's control.

Since the catcher will develop more bad habits in practice than in games, we work on the premise that perfect practice makes perfect games.

We know that most catchers will not wear any gear when they warm up pitchers in the bull pen and will shy away from balls in the dirt. So when they catch batting practice you can expect them to make little or no attempt to block such balls. That is their habit pattern.

That's why we have our catchers wear their gear in the bull pen and catch batting practice just as they would in a game. (Warning: Catching too much batting practice can do more harm than good.) We also feel it is important to block all the balls in the dirt, whether there are runners on base or not. This develops the right kind of instincts and is also psychologically beneficial to the pitcher.

It is essential to conduct the practice drills at a level that will produce results. A coach should never, out of emotion or frustration, increase the intensity of a drill to the point of no return. Whenever the athletes are not getting the job done in practice, he must back off and create an environment in which the athlete can achieve some success. Success breeds success.

We start our catchers with a no-glove drill, blocking half-speed fastballs in the dirt. The catcher must clasp his hands behind his back and try to block the ball with quickness and body position. The hands behind the back force the catcher to concentrate on the block rather than on trying to catch the ball.

SURROUNDING THE BALL.

CATCHING

Ironically, the receiver will probably catch more balls when he is trying to block them than he will when he is actually trying to catch the ball.

The shadow drill, using a ball on a stick, offers another good lead-up device. The coach sets up in front of the catcher and moves the ball to the catcher's right, left, and in front of him. The catcher reacts by shifting his body and hands into the proper position to block the ball. The coach can simulate both fastballs and curveballs.

A ground-ball drill can be used to help teach the idea of keeping the hands down when blocking the ball rather than lifting them to catch it. The catcher, wearing full gear, deploys well back in the infield, and we fungo ground balls at or near him, which he must block. He cannot reach out or up to catch the ball no matter how hard or slowly the ball is hit.

This drill requires a great deal of discipline, as the catcher must follow the ball for over 100 feet and resist the instinct to field the infield grounder.

Once the catcher has developed his technique from the work in the bull pen and batting practice, we proceed to a block and reach drill. This is a dual-purpose drill in which we have base runners trying to advance on balls that elude the catcher.

We want our catcher to block the ball, retrieve it, and get into throwing position without looking to see if the runner is advancing.

In short, he must assume that the runner will try to advance on every ball in the dirt. If the runner doesn't go, the catcher must be informed by his teammates.

What does the catcher do when the ball goes into the dirt and a runner is stealing? The answer depends upon the distance from plate to backstop, game situation (outs, innings, score), catcher's arm, and the runner's speed.

Our basic concern is the distance from plate to backstop. If it is not too far (generally 60 feet or less), we try to move into the ball, short-hop it, and throw to 2B or 3B. We feel that even if the ball gets by the catcher, the close backstop will prevent the runner from advancing more than one base on the steal. Once the catcher goes to his knees to block the ball, he will lose the chance to throw the runner out.

In conclusion, remember this: No one in his right mind will instinctively put his body in front of an object thrown 90 miles per hour. The instinct is to get out of the way or pick up your hands to protect yourself.

Hence, for the catcher to achieve success in handling balls in the dirt a coach must reverse a natural impulse, and this can be done only through repeated practice under game conditions.

Help your defense, help your pitcher, and help your catcher by concentrating on blocking balls in the dirt.

THROWING

Most catchers build up a reputation by their ability to throw people out. With lots of help from our pitchers, our goal is to throw out 60 percent of the runners who attempt to steal. To do this we have to consistently be able to throw accurately to 2B in 2.0 seconds or less.

Throwing is a function of stance, footwork, loading (readjusting to throw), grip, and release.

The key factor in throwing is to have a stance that allows for quickness and the ability to generate momentum toward the base we are throwing to.

Momentum is a key factor, and that is where footwork comes into play. Our footwork must get us clear of the batter and get us moving in the direction of the throw. All momentum starts with the right foot moving first no matter where the pitch is. (The obvious exception would be on a ball way behind a right-handed batter with a runner stealing 2B.) The momentum step with the right foot is a short quick shuffle while keeping the right foot at a 45° angle to a line directly from the mound to home. The momentum step with the right foot is accompanied by a quick step toward 2B with the left foot. This total action produces a modified jump-pivot action, which should occur just as we catch the ball, not after.

The ball inside to a right-handed batter should be surrounded by the glove with all the momentum going toward 2B. The ball away from the right-hander should be handled by starting with a right-foot step up and out so that we catch the ball with our head slightly on the 1B side of the ball.

The ball inside to a left-handed batter can be handled one of two ways. One, we can move up and out away from the left-handed batter on our right-foot step as we catch the ball. Two, we can step laterally across with our right foot and center in front of the ball as we catch it and then clear the batter by taking another step up and away from the batter with the right foot. The rhythm would be right, catch, right, left, throw. The first technique is much faster but risky. The technique we will use will depend upon arm strength, the type of pitch, the running speed of the runner at 1B, and the game situation (inning, outs, score, and runners on 1B and 3B).

There are other footwork techniques to clear the batter and to gain momentum. The key is finding the technique that allows the individual catcher to reach his maximum efficiency.

THE MOMENTUM STEP WITH THE RIGHT FOOT IS ACCOMPANIED BY A QUICK STEP TOWARD 2B WITH THE LEFT FOOT.

In a running situation we must anticipate that the runner is going on every pitch. We must ready ourselves by staying down and moving into the ball and catching the ball close to our body. If we reach out for the ball, we have to bring it back in when we load into a throwing position. The ball moves faster than our hands can move. We basically catch the ball into our body and take it out of our shirt pocket to throw. This produces a short arm swing. The exception is the ball into a right-handed batter which we will sweep into a throwing position.

Our throwing hand should not drop below our waist to get our arm up to a throwing position. Our glove pushes the ball straight up to a throwing

THE BALL SHOULD BE RELEASED WITH THE LEGS BENT.

THE ARM SHOULD BE EXTENDED WHEN THROWING.   NO LONG FOLLOW-THROUGH IS NECESSARY

CATCHING

position with the elbow about as high as the shoulder (not below). The throwing hand should be away from the head with the elbow at about a 90° angle. The ball must be directly above the hand before we release it to insure the proper backspin rotation. To facilitate getting to a high pitch above the hand position, we should use the glove to push the ball straight back, with our throwing fingers on top of the ball and our shoulders rotated so the lead shoulder points directly toward 2B.

The proper grip will contribute to the best rotation and carry, plus it will make the throw easier to handle. The grip should be firm across the wide seams with the index and middle fingers slightly spread and the thumb underneath. The grip should be adjusted as we are loading to a throwing position. When we are ready to release, the glove drops down to allow for the release.

The ball should be released with the legs bent. The lower the pitch the more the leg flex. The arm should be extended when throwing. The wrist snaps at the last moment. When the release is finished, your throwing arm will be directly in line with the target. No long extended follow-through is necessary.

We can throw from a ¾ or sidearm position, but the ball should be released overhand whenever possible. Sometimes, especially on a ball low and away from a right-handed batter or when our throw is tailing too much, we must tilt our head to the left so that we force ourselves into a more over-hand position.

We must fine center (small-target focus) on our target, making sure to keep our eyes on the target until the ball gets there. Our eyes should not pick up the ball in flight. Our targets will vary depending upon conditions.

In throwing to 3B we need not start our momentum until we see the runner going. The most important factor is to clear the batter. We cannot put ourselves in a position where we have to throw through the batter. Again we are going to start everything with our right foot. The pitch will dictate where we step. We don't need to deal with a left-handed batter since we have a clear shot. If the ball is away from a right-handed batter, we need to step up and out with our right foot and throw in front of the batter. If the ball is over the middle of the plate or inside to a right-handed batter, we will step left and throw behind the batter. On either pitch we should start our throw slightly toward the third baseline side of 3B. We do this to compensate for the slight change in momentum we have to make when throwing to 3B. Usually, when we make a bad throw to 3B it is in to the runner, so we are just overcompensating.

Any time the batter's swing brings him across the plate or he hinders us in any way, it is important we go through with our throw and force as much contact with the batter as we can. Sometimes it calls for a good acting job.

You can improve your throwing by throwing. Play lots of long catch. Throw on your knees straight on and sideways. Paint or tape a stripe on a ball across the wide seams. If you can see the stripe clearly when you throw, you are probably throwing the ball with good backspin rotation. Pull-ups (hands over and close together), tricep extensions, hand grips, and surgical tubing will strengthen those muscles you use to throw. Get yourself in good cardiovascular condition; run long distance as well as sprints.

FRAMING THE PLATE

Most coaches are satisfied if they can put a player behind the plate who wants to catch, can throw, and will catch the ball. If the individual has those three attributes, there is probably very little time spent on the technique of catching the ball. However, just catching the ball is not enough. How the catcher catches greatly affects the pitcher's performance and the outcome of the game.

Our goal is not to have balls called strikes but to have every strike called a strike. We especially want the marginal strike, the "stri-ball," called a strike. This is the ball on the corners, the pitch just at or slightly below the knees, the fastball just above the waist, and the curveball at the waist. How we catch this pitch determines whether it will be called a ball or a strike. Would you rather hit with a 3-1 count or a 2-2? The answer is obvious, but how this applies to the catcher is not. If we catch the 2-1 stri-ball correctly, it is a strike and the count is 2-2; if not, it's a ball and the count is 3-1. Poor catching also puts the pitcher in jeopardy of throwing too many pitches. The more pitches the hitters see, the better chance they have of making solid contact. Also, those extra pitches wear out the pitcher's arm.

Good catching starts with the glove. A one-break glove is best since it allows for maximum control of the glove in backhanding the outside pitch. The entire hand should not be in the glove. The heel of the hand should be slightly out of the glove to preserve wrist flexibility. An inflexible wrist leads to dropped pitches, and any time you drop a pitch you can't hope that it will be called a strike. The heel of the hand can be protected by a leather extension laced onto the heel of the glove with a piece of foam rubber glued on the backside.

Dropped pitches are also often the result of the catcher blinking as the ball arrives at the plate. This can be overcome by consciously blinking as the ball is released by the pitcher. Some catchers drop pitches because they duck their head as the hitter swings. This can be remedied during batting practice with a little help from a video or super-8 film.

We like a wide-based stance with the feet spread slightly wider than the shoulders and the toes slightly pointed out. The hips should be above the knees with the back flat or near flat. The catcher should position himself as close to the batter as he can without interfering. The hands should be held out away from the body with the arms flexed and the elbows pointed out.

If the arms are too straight, the glove hand and wrist become too stiff. If the hands are too far back, they meet the ball too far from the plate. The elbows should be out to allow lateral movement of the glove hand. The bare hand should be held flat behind the glove with the thumb tucked behind the index finger. The bare hand may also be held behind the right knee or back in non-running situations. Many coaches prefer the loose fist, but this exposes the knuckles, and many catchers extend their fingers when they catch the ball, giving rise to split fingers. If the catcher's hand is flat and it happens to be exposed to a foul tip, chances are he will not split a finger or damage a knuckle.

The ball must be met in the strike zone, not received and taken away from the plate. The pitch is more of a strike the closer it is caught to the plate; it is less of a strike the farther away it is caught. In catching the ball, the glove frames the perimeter of the strike zone on close pitches. The ball

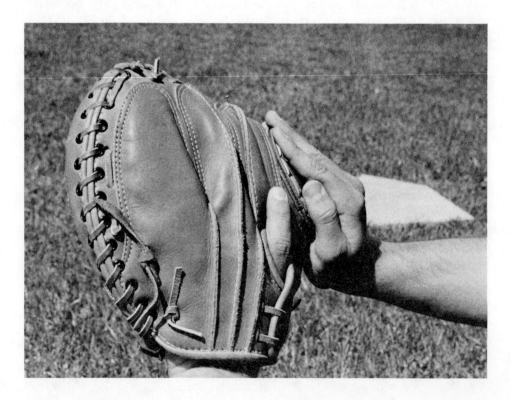

BARE HAND SHOULD BE HELD FLAT BEHIND THE GLOVE WITH THE THUMB TUCKED BEHIND THE INDEX FINGER.

on the inside corner to a right-handed hitter should be caught with the glove facing into the plate, as opposed to the glove facing the pitcher. If the inside pitch is caught with the glove facing the pitcher, the umpire views the majority of the glove outside the strike zone. Whereas, if on the inside-corner pitch the glove is facing into the plate, the umpire can see the ball and see that the ball is on the corner.

The ball on the outside corner of the plate to the right-handed hitter should be backhanded so that the glove faces into the plate. This backhand technique keeps the ball in the strike zone where the umpire can see it. It also allows for maximum glove surface to catch the ball. If this pitch is caught palm up across your body, chances are it will be dropped due to lack of glove surface, or if it is caught, it will probably be carried out of the strike zone. Any time a strike is dropped or made to look like a ball, the umpire's tendency is to call it a ball.

The low ball (at the knees or slightly below) should be caught with the glove facing up and the wrist bent slightly toward the catcher. The low ball caught with the glove face down pushes it down out of the strike zone. Catching the low ball with the glove face up but the top of the glove tilted down makes the low ball look lower than it really is. The high ball should be caught with the glove face down. If the high ball is caught with the glove facing the pitcher, the ball appears to the umpire to be 8–10 inches above where it really is because the umpire sees the back of the glove which extends above the ball. Balls that are both high and inside or outside, or low and inside or outside can be framed by tilting the glove to an in-between position.

In a non-running situation it is critical to let the close pitch sit. Too many catchers raise up to return the ball to the pitcher or to the third baseman on a third strike. If the umpire is unsure as to whether a pitch is a ball or a strike and the catcher bounces up, the tendency is to call the pitch a ball. Conversely, if you let the pitch sit, the umpire may call it a strike, and if he doesn't call that one a strike he'll probably adjust and call the next one a strike.

In letting the ball sit, timing is critical. The pitch should be held still where it is met long enough for the umpire to have a good clear look at it, but not so long that he feels that you are trying to coerce him into calling it a strike. Umpires are taking more time in calling pitches. Don't rush them by picking up your glove too soon. If they are rushed, umpires will call a strike a ball before they'll call a ball a strike. One way of insuring that your catcher will not raise up too soon on the close strike is to have him throw the ball back to the pitcher by going to his knees with no runners on base.

Every pitch in or near the strike zone should be caught with a minimum of body movement. We tell our catchers to shrink the strike zone with

FRAMING THE PLATE: IN ALL FOUR PHOTOGRAPHS, THE CATCHER ON THE LEFT IS DEMONSTRATING PROPER TECHNIQUE.

FRAMING THE PLATE: IN ALL FOUR PHOTOGRAPHS, THE CATCHER ON THE RIGHT IS DEMONSTRATING IMPROPER TECHNIQUE.

their hands. We liken it to picking fruit off a tree. The ball should be caught with very smooth hand action. We do not want to jerk or pull any pitches into the strike zone. Remember, we want only those strikes we are entitled to. Good framing technique will usually get you more marginal pitches. We are not trying to put one over on the umpire, only to give our strikes the best showcase possible. If you are not smooth, the umpire will feel that you are trying to take advantage of him by pulling pitches into the strike zone, and he could take pitches away from you.

In running situations, our priority is on throwing people out, and the framing aspect is secondary. Instead of catching the ball up to the plate, we catch the ball back into our body so it is easier to load and throw.

We develop our catching skills by starting without a glove and catching tennis balls. This forces the catcher to use his hand and fingers in controlling the glove. It gets him away from relying on the glove to snag the ball. This no-glove technique also allows the coach and catcher to evaluate hand position in relation to the plate. We progress from no glove with tennis balls to using a glove and catching tennis balls. Tennis balls are very bouncy and will rebound from the glove if the catcher does not really bear down on catching the ball firmly. He is catching the ball two-handed with one hand. After the ball hits the glove, the bare hand covers the glove to secure the ball. Catchers who catch with their bare hand behind the back or knee will basically catch everything with one hand. We quite naturally progress to baseballs, catching pitches in the bull pen, and then batting practice. During the learning process we catch a minimum of batting practice and thereafter no more than 10 minutes at a stretch so as not to develop bad habits due to fatigue.

Catch strikes, and remember you win with the stri-ball if you frame the plate.

CATCHING

THE CATCHER MUST BE A TAKE-CHARGE GUY. IT'S HIS SHOW, AND HE MUST RUN THE GAME AND HIS CLUB CORRECTLY. *IT TAKES GUTS TO CATCH PLUS A GOOD KNOWLEDGEABLE HEAD.*

FUNDAMENTALS OF CATCHING:

CATCHER MUST REMIND PITCHER:

1. When fielding bunts, where to throw.

2. When starting double play, who's covering second.

3. On balls hit to right side, break toward first.

4. To back up third and home plate when throw is coming to those bases.

5. Of the score and the number and importance of out.

CATCHER MUST REMIND THIRD BASEMAN:

1. Speed of runner.

2. When bunt is in order.

3. To be cutoff man on single to left when man is on second.

4. When going for double play and letting one run score.

5. Amount of room third baseman has when going for any pop fly.

6. Give inside target to third baseman when man is scoring so that third baseman will not hit runner.

CATCHER MUST REMIND FIRST BASEMAN:

1. Speed of runner.

2. When bunt is in order.

3. When base runners may be stealing.

4. When to be cutoff man and where to be standing.

5. Importance of tying and winning runs.

6. Amount of room first baseman has when going for pop flys.

CATCHER MUST REMIND PITCHER:

1. Pick up target.

2. Concentrate.

3. Use some deception in motion, etc.

4. Pitch low.

5. Follow through and bend back.

6. Shove off back leg and drive toward home plate.

7. Change speeds.

8. Don't be a thrower.

9. Think about what he is doing.

GIVING SIGNS:

SQUAT POSITION—RIGHT KNEE AT PITCHER.
RIGHT WRIST CLOSE TO GROIN.
GLOVE HAND EXTENDS OVER LEFT KNEE WITH POCKET
  FACING PLATE.

1. Position glove to block vision of coaches.

2. Hold glove in same position whether fastball or curve.

CATCHING

3. Think of situation, what needed, ground ball, etc.

4. When in tough spot, use pitcher's best pitch.

5. Don't be afraid to pitch out when you think runner may be going or when you want to attempt to pick someone off.

6. Don't give signs in too big a hurry—think out situation.

7. Don't give so low that on-deck hitter can see signs between your legs.

8. Finger signs 1-2-3-4. These are used most of the time for fastball, curve, change, and extra pitch or pitchout.

9. Flap sign up, down, and wiggle. Signs are usually changed with runner on 2B or if pitcher has trouble seeing signs.

AFTER GIVING SIGN, YOU NOW BECOME A RECEIVER:

1. Stay low.

2. Don't have your tail way up in the air.

3. Don't have your tail dragging on the ground.

4. Spread your legs.

5. Bend arms slightly in a relaxed fashion.

6. Give pitcher a good target.

7. Left foot up in front slightly.

8. Point toes out.

9. Stay on balls of your feet; catch on heels.

10. Keep elbows out from in-between legs.

11. Keep arms out for freedom.

DON'T:

1. Become a jumping jack and jump up in front of umpire. (Stay low.)

2. Snap or jab at ball. Receive the ball gracefully—let the ball come to you.

3. Bring ball into strike zone.

4. Move up on curveball.

5. Move back on fastball. (Stay in same position.)

WITH RUNNERS ON BASE:

1. Look on every runner as a base stealer.

2. Be alert and catch all thrown balls. Don't let anything get by, especially with man on base.

3. Think. Anticipate when the steal may be in order.

4. Put weight on left foot, then shift weight to back foot.

5. Create rhythm when catching ball, bring glove and hand back together, swaying shoulders.

6. Take ball out of glove as glove and hand come back, cock wrist, and throw from over the top.

7. Grip ball across seams for accuracy.

8. Keep bottom horizontal to the ground, down just slightly.

9. Don't be afraid to pitch out.

10. Don't be afraid to try to pick a runner off. This will depend on score, outs, etc.

11. Assume stance as close to batter as possible.

12. Do not take too many steps when releasing ball—it is more of a pivot than a step.

SHIFTING WHEN RUNNERS GOING:

1. Pitch to right, step with right foot.

2. Pitch to left, step with left foot.

3. When step is to the left and throw is necessary, bring right foot behind left.

4. Anticipate the shifting more so when calling for breaking pitches.

5. Use the left foot as a guide and step to base you are throwing to.

ALL CATCHERS SHOULD:

1. Block balls in dirt by falling to knees.

2. Keep runners close to bases by attempting pickoffs.

3. Field ground balls and taps in front of plate by using two hands.

4. Throw bat out of way when play is coming into home plate.

WHEN CATCHING POP FLYS:

1. Remember to throw mask off and out of way.

2. Make certain palms up. All pop flys out in front of home plate will come down like right-hander's curveball and will go away. Turn around and let ball come into your chest.

3. Go to fence and screen areas then come away to catch pop-ups—ball will come back.

4. On pop flys in front of home plate you should turn in front of plate with your back to the pitcher's mound, as the spin of the ball will make it come back toward the mound.

5. On pops to your left, you will turn to your left, and on pops to your right, you will turn to your right.

CATCHING DRILLS FOR IMPROVEMENT:

1. Keep equipment on during most agility drills.

2. Two catchers throw low balls in dirt to each other, 60 feet. (Drop to knees to block ball.)

3. Two catchers throw balls on short hop to each other, 100 feet (relax arms, let ball come to you).

4. Throw in squatting position to second base, repetition will be necessary.

5. Make imaginary tags in front of home plate with all balls thrown home during infield practice.

6. Field topped balls out in front of home plate using glove as scoop.

7. Step with front foot to bag you are throwing to at all times.

8. Bring both glove and arm back with rhythm when throwing.

9. Get in the habit of throwing with fingers across seams; set ball in glove.

10. Stay behind home plate when throwing in infield practice.

11. Throw long distances to strengthen arm.

12. Field balls in foul territory and make throws to 1B and 3B on blocked balls.

13. Imaginary first and third situations: look runner back at 3B, then throw through to 2B or 3B. If runner at first is tying or winning run, ignore glance to 3B and throw to 2B with maximum effort.

14. Stance is important. Practice staying on balls of feet, feet open, pointing out, and left leg and foot up in front of right leg.

15. Practice receiving ball. Let ball come to you, don't jab.

16. Frame plate when warming pitchers up. This will get you into habit when game starts.

17. Make pitcher work when warming him up. Remember you are preparing him for game and not just playing catch.

18. Catching batting practice is an important drill. Use it wisely, don't be lazy.

19. THE MOST IMPORTANT DRILL OF ALL IS TO TRAIN YOURSELF TO THINK . . . THINK . . . THINK . . . THINK . . . THINK. . . .

FIELDING

PICKOFF PLAYS

BELOW ARE EXPLAINED THE SIMPLEST PICKOFF PLAYS. ALL CAN BE EXECUTED WITH REPETITIOUS PRACTICE. ON ALL PICKOFF PLAYS TIMING IS THE KEY.

THE DAYLIGHT PLAY:

This play is put into effect by the shortstop and pitcher. The shortstop must jockey himself back and forth behind the runner on 2B. Each time he goes back and forth he gets a little closer to 2B. When the pitcher has finally taken his position on the mound and has come to his set position (hands resting in the belt area and relaxed), he will then look to 2B, and should he see there is daylight between the runner and the shortstop, the pitcher now knows that the signal for picking the man off at second is in order. As soon as the pitcher sees the daylight he sets his head and says to himself, "one-thousand," turns, and throws to 2B. The shortstop who knows there is daylight between himself and the runner immediately breaks for the bag.

CATCHER CALLING PICKOFF BY USING FINGER SIGNS:

This pickoff play, is usually called by the catcher, but also can be called by an infielder who, in turn, gives the sign to the catcher. Catcher at all times must give sign to the pitcher to advise him play is in order.

When the catcher, infielder, or pitcher has determined that a runner is getting too far off any of the bases then an indicator sign between them is given. This can be a variety of motions (pick ear, touch top of cap, etc.). When the pitcher acknowledges the sign, the catcher will, depending upon which base the play will go to, use his fingers accordingly. He will indicate to the pitcher the following: One finger, 1B; two fingers, 2B with second baseman covering; three fingers, 2B with shortstop covering; four fingers, 3B. Now that the pitcher has the sign and knows what base he is going to, both he and the infielder must now watch the catcher's clenched right hand which is resting on the catcher's right knee. The pitcher, who has come to a set position on the mound will turn and throw to the proper base when he sees the clenched fist open. The infielder, who also has been watching the clenched fist on the right knee, will break to the bag as he sees the clenched fist open.

PICKOFF PLAY AT FIRST BASE BETWEEN FIRST BASEMAN AND PITCHER:

This play is used when it's an obvious bunt situation and the first baseman is holding the runner on first. Should a pitch be a ball or hit foul, a good time to call this play is on the very next pitch. It can be set into action by the first baseman going to the mound and telling the pitcher or it can be called with a sign between them both. The manager can also call this play from the bench.

EXAMPLE: Man on 1B and bunt in order. First baseman holding man on, pitcher comes to set position, throws pitch to home plate, and it is a ball or fouled off. On the very next pitch, after sign is given, first baseman will charge two hard steps like he is going in to pick up bunt. He stops after his two hard steps and returns to 1B to put tag on runner. Pitcher will have to hold ball a second and give the first baseman time to get back. Just a short hesitation is all that is needed as most times runner has taken big lead off bag.

REMINDER: NOT ALL PITCHERS HAVE THE QUICKNESS IN THEIR PICKOFF MOVES OR THE MENTAL ALERTNESS.

ALL PITCHERS SHOULD BE TAUGHT AND DRILLED, BUT UNDER GAME CONDITIONS, THE CATCHER SHOULD DETERMINE WHAT PITCHERS ARE QUALIFIED TO MAKE THE PICKOFF PLAYS WORK . . .

SEQUENCE PLAY

Two possibilities exist for defending against a bunt with men on 1B and 2B.

1.   This play depends upon pitcher throwing strike. Play can be set up by either first baseman, third baseman, or manager . . . use a signal or go to mound and tell pitcher.

On the first pitch, just as the pitcher gets set and readies himself to throw, the third baseman will break in hard to field bunt, the shortstop will go to 3B for putout, the second baseman will go to 2B for possible play there. The first baseman will stay on the bag, and the pitcher will cover all bunted balls on 1B side.

Should a ball be bunted extremely hard, there is always the possibility of getting a double play on this play.

2.   The reverse of this play can be done on the opposite side and will depend upon who is hitting on opposite club. If a left-hand hitter or player known to bunt to the right side only is up, the first baseman charges in hard for bunted ball, second baseman covers first base, shortstop covers 2B, and third baseman stays at 3B. Pitcher's job is to cover 3B side.

With runners on first and second the bunt will usually go to the 3B side. This being the case, the defense will most times be having the third baseman charge.

These plays are not difficult to execute as long as the pitcher throws strikes.

Catcher at all times will call the base play is to be made to.

THE RUNDOWN PLAY

1. You must make every attempt to run the runner back toward the base he came from.

2. Try to begin the rundown play when the runner is halfway between the bases.

3. Once the forward man receives the ball let him run the runner back to the bag from which he came.

4. The forward man, with ball held in high throwing position, should run at the runner.

5. Both defensive players should be on the same side of runner so throw will not have to cross and possibly hit runner.

6. Tagger should stay inside the baseline and a few feet in front of the bag.

7. When runner is about 10 feet from tagger, the tagger will move forward and say to the other defensive player "now." The other player will then throw the ball, and the tag will then be made.

8. With perfect execution there should only be one throw.

STARTING POINTS FOR PROPER FIELDING

1. Foot spread depends upon most comfortable position for individual infielder but not too wide.

2. Toes should be pointed out.

3. Keep weight on balls of feet.

4. Knees slightly bent.

5. Body leaning forward.

6. Hands off knees.

7. Body in semi-crouch.

8. As pitcher releases ball, move slightly to get body going (6-inch shuffle step).

9. Lay glove open as you come into ball.

10. Do not wait until last second to open glove up. This will cause flipping action.

11. Center the ball in the middle of your body.

12. Try to get in front of every ball. When not possible, don't be afraid to backhand the ball.

13. Keep your tail low at all times.

14. Lay glove on the ground—let ball roll into it.

15. Keep your head down and watch ball go into glove.

16. Keep off your heels and go to ball.

17. Charge everything you can.

18. Have relaxed hands. Do not jab or be stiff with glove. Relax.

19. On ball hit to infielder's throwing side, make sure back leg and foot are thrown out and shoved along top of dirt with sliding action when about to catch ball, then plant back leg.

20. Infielder must establish in his mind his weak and strong side. He then must lean toward side he doesn't go well to until this is improved.

21. Whether infielder plays deep or shallow is determined by infielder's evaluation of his own arm and range.

22. It is most times easier to go to glove side.

23. A crossover step should be used when a lateral movement is necessary.

24. When fielding ground ball, keep hands out in front of body. Don't field ball with hands in close.

25. On bad hops the infielder should act rather than react. Never let the ball play you.

26. Catch the ball when it is to your advantage. Infielder should try to catch ball on short hop whenever possible.

27. Keep hands below the ball.

28. Remember a ball will come up more than it will down—stay low.

29. GET AS MANY GROUND BALLS AS POSSIBLE. INFIELDERS ARE MADE AT THE OTHER END OF A FUNGO STICK.

BASIC INFIELD PROCEDURES

BE A GENERAL AND TAKE CHARGE OF YOUR OWN INDI-
VIDUAL POSITION. EVERY INFIELDER SHOULD:

1. Be repetitious in all infield practice drills.

2. Repeat over and over in mind, "Every ball hit will be hit to me."
    There is no doubt it will happen.

3. Know what to do with ball before it is hit to you.

4. Determine speed of ball. This will help determine what base to
    throw to.

5. Determine upon going to left or right what base will be easiest
    for play being made.

6. Know the outs and innings.

7. Know the hitter and play him correctly (pull, straight away, or
    opposite field).

8. Use infield practice as a tool to help better yourself. Don't be
    nonchalant.

9. Throw from longer distances. This will stretch out arm for relays,
    as well as strengthen it in general.

10. Use pepper practice for bettering agility and quickness of hands.
    Don't use more than three players, and spread them out.

11. Know the pitch so you can shade hitter a specific way. Tell other
    infielder with word sign to prepare him (shortstop tell third base-
    man; second baseman tell first baseman).

12. Go back for all pop flys until outfielder runs you off. They are
    your balls until you hear him—then get out of way.

13. Run catchers off most pop flys. It is much easier for you coming in and without catching gear on.

14. Make sure of getting head man when double play is in order.

15. Infielder catching ground ball catches ball; second man on other end of double play is man that executes it.

16. Make sure good throw is given to executor. Don't hide ball.

17. Make certain ground ball hit is really double-play ball. Many double plays are mishandled because ball was really not hit fast enough for double play to be completed in the first place.

18. Know the range of the infielder next to you.

19. Know the arm strength of the outfielders. This will determine how far out you must go when acting as cutoff man.

20. Know the running speed of hitter.

21. Stay with ball. Should you boot ball, there is always the chance of catching runner if you come up with ball second time.

22. MAKE CERTAIN THAT YOU SEE ALL OPPOSING BASE RUNNERS TAG THE BAGS.

THROWING

1. Accuracy is the most important part of throwing.

2. Using good fundamentals in throwing practice will develop accuracy.

3. Every time a ball is thrown between two people, a spot should be picked out and the player should throw to it.

4. Don't just throw for the sake of warming up. Throw for improved accuracy.

5. For accuracy and better carry, get in the habit of throwing from over the top.

6. When possible, set fingers across the seams.

7. Infielders, outfielders, and catchers should follow through with their throws just as pitchers. Bring your arm through.

8. All plays in the infield cannot be made from coming over top. At times the infielder as well as catcher may have to come from side for execution. Be smart enough to know when this is necessary. Against a fast runner or when a play will be extremely close, fielder must realize he does not have enough time to bring arm up to top throwing position.

9. Throw extended distances to develop arm strength.

10. Charging a ground ball will help get a better and harder throw off.

11. Infielders, outfielders, and catchers: Forget warming up with knuckle- and curveballs.

INFIELD DRILLS FOR IMPROVEMENT

1. Get as many ground balls hit to you as possible.

2. Use infield practice as a tool to make you better. It's not just something to do before the game starts.

3. Play in a pepper game as much as possible, two to a game.

4. In pepper games use one hand.

5. Skip rope for agility and quickness.

6. Get body moving to improve range.

7. Spread out and do long pickups with another infielder, throwing ground balls.

8. Put light weights on ankles for a short period when fielding ground balls.

9. Practice double plays over and over.

10. Throw at extended distance to stretch out arm and improve strength.

11. Pick out a spot and throw to it when playing catch with other infielder.

12. Third baseman: get slow throws to you on sidelines just as if topped ball. Come in and pick this ball up in a semi-arc bare-handed. Grab down on ball just as if you were going to shove it in ground.

13. Practice the crossover step even when not fielding ball. Imagine ball to both right and left.

FIELDING

14. Throw ball underhanded with other infielder. Keep wrist stiff, just as if double play is being made. This can be done on sidelines as well as during infield practice.

15. When playing catch or playing pepper let your hands relax. Get the feeling of ball coming into your hands softly. Don't jab or be stiff.

16. Shortstop or second baseman should not get too big a glove. Use a glove that you can handle and not one that is difficult to get ball out of.

17. Catch as many pop flys as possible.

18. Practice going back on ball. Kick self in tail to be in position to field ball with back to outfield.

19. Practice going to weak side.

TAGGING THE RUNNER

1. Straddle the bag.

2. Have ball in glove, close glove tight, and tag with back of glove hand.

3. Never show runner ball.

4. On close play, take glove down and right back up.

5. Always make umpire feel you know runner was out.

6. Stay with sliding base runner. Many times he will come off the bag.

7. Watch for slider sliding away from bag and coming in with hand.

8. Fake runner by standing straight up with hands on sides as if there will be no play on him. He may slow down and be tagged out (this play more times at 3B than at 2B).

FIRST BASE

FIRST BASEMAN HAS THREE POSITIONS HE MUST TAKE. WHICH POSITION WILL BE TAKEN DEPENDS UPON THE SITUATION:

1. INNING.   Late in game hold lead run close to first.

2. SCORE.   With comfortable lead play back to get out.

3. OUTS. With 2 outs can play deep, unless holding fast runner at first.

4. HITTER.   Shade according to hitter's pulling ability. Determine depth based on hitter's speed and threat to drag bunt.

DEEP POSITION:

1. Strong left-hand hitter.

2. Guard foul line when extra base hit will allow runner to score.

HALFWAY:

1. Over to right with right-hand hitter hitting.

2. When bunt or push-bunt hitter hitting.

IF THROW IS TO RIGHT, LEFT-HANDED FIRST BASEMAN PUTS LEFT FOOT ON BAG.

FIRST BASE

IN:

1. When bunt definitely in order.

FIRST BASEMAN SHOULD:

1. Switch feet on thrown ball if this is natural.

    EXAMPLE: LH–1B — Throw to right, left foot on bag.
    Throw to left, right foot on bag.
    RH–1B — Throw to left, right foot on bag.
    Throw to right, left foot on bag, glove
    crossover.
    Throw directly in center—either foot acceptable.

2. No need to switch feet, however. Go to corner of bag in the direction throw is coming. Stretch and push off back leg.

3. By always pushing off back leg (left-handed thrower, left leg, right-handed thrower, right leg), first baseman will get maximum reach.

4. Get in the habit of using one hand.

5. Block all bad throws.

6. Remind pitcher when runner is taking too big a lead.

7. When tagging runner coming down line on a bad throw, do not jab at runner but follow around with glove after tag has been made. Let runner tag himself out.

8. When practicing to improve one-handed play, put throwing hand in back pocket and use only glove hand. Confidence will be built this way.

9. Knock all ground balls down. Lie in front of them and fall on knees if necessary. First base is close by, so play can always be made.

10. Get in habit of taking every throw as far out as you can. Don't catch ball in by chest; stretch out at all times. Don't let throw ride in.

11. Give pitcher good target for pickoff play.

12. Don't be afraid to come off bag to make a play. This is a judgment play, and you will have to determine if you can get back in time.

13. Determine the range of second baseman.

14. Get all plays you can going to your right.

15. Yield to second baseman if play is easier for him.

16. Call pitchers and catchers off all pop flys that are easier for you to make. Go to fence and screens, then come away to make catch.

17. When acting as cutoff man, hold hands up high giving good target.

18. When acting as cutoff man and throw is coming from center field, get up in front of mound so that throw won't hit mound or rubber and take a crazy hop.

19. Always hustle to get yourself in cutoff position early.

20. Do not get too close to home plate as cutoff man. No value if too near.

21. When holding man on, after pitcher has delivered ball, get into a fielding position.

22. Have body as much as possible in fair territory when holding man on; it doesn't do any good making a good play on foul ball.

23. Listen for catcher's command when acting as cutoff man.

24. Keep throw out of line of runner when making throw to 2B for double play. Keep throw on outfield side of the bag. Take a step up or back depending upon time and speed of ball hit.

25. Make accurate throws.

26. When it is necessary for pitcher to cover 1B, give pitcher ball as soon as possible.

27. Give pitcher a firm underhand throw. Stiff wrist will aid accuracy.

28. Follow flight of ball to pitcher. Should he drop ball, then you will be near to make play.

29. Advise pitchers of other runners on base should they try to advance.

30. Follow runner to 2B on sure double when second baseman or shortstop must act as cutoff man.

31. Guard foul line when extra-base hit means an important run.

32. Run pitcher off topped balls, etc., when easier for you to make play.

33. Shout to catcher, "There he goes" when runner is stealing.

34. Make as many putouts as possible yourself when fielding ground balls. Don't take the chance of handling ball twice.

35. Know when bunt is in order and charge ball.

IN EXECUTING DOUBLE PLAY, TAG BAG WITH LEFT FOOT AND SHOVE OFF ONTO RIGHT AS TAG IS BEING MADE.

SECOND BASE

THE FIELDING FUNDAMENTALS SET FORTH ON PREVIOUS PAGES LARGELY APPLY TO THE SECOND BASEMAN. HOWEVER, THERE ARE OTHER SPECIFICS THAT THE SECOND BASEMAN SHOULD DO:

1. Knock the ball down at all times; yours is a short throw.

2. On a hard-hit ground ball, no one on, don't be afraid to drop to the right knee.

3. Establish the range of the first baseman. Run him off most balls to your left.

4. Your throw will most times be a ¾-type throw. When acting as a relay man and when making throws home, however, stay up on top for better accuracy as well as carry.

5. Don't get in the habit of flipping the ball. Arm strength cannot be developed this way.

6. Verbally keep your shortstop, first baseman, and pitcher alive.

7. Communicate with shortstop about who is covering bag. Let shortstop determine this by hiding mouth with glove, using closed mouth to mean me, and open mouth to mean you.

8. Anticipate at all times what you are going to do with ball before it is hit to you.

9. On ball hit to your right, throw out right leg and slide along top of dirt as going to ball. As ball is fielded, plant right foot and throw against it.

10. Cover 1B when bunt is in order.

11. Make every effort to get to pop fly down right-field line that first baseman can't get.

12. Go back on all pop flys until outfielders run you off.

13. Do not play too deep—you must cheat on double play as well as when covering bag for steals.

14. When covering 1B on bunt, go to bag and play bag as first baseman would. Don't time it to just barely get there. Be there early to give a target.

15. When covering the bag for defense of the double steal, go directly to bag and listen for the verbal command from the shortstop. If the runner on 3B is going for home, you will have to come up from the bag and make your throw home. If the runner stays, then you must lay back and tag runner out.

IN MAKING THE DOUBLE PLAY:

1. Do not feel that every ball hit with a man on is a double-play ball. Speed of ball and where ball is hit will determine this.

2. Always get the head man. Your job is first to catch the ball, then to give shortstop a good throw. The shortstop will execute the double play.

3. Shortstop will cover all balls hit back to pitcher unless a real dead right-handed pull hitter is hitting. It will then be your responsibility.

4. This can change, however, if it is established that shortstop has a real weak arm. In that case, you will make this play.

5. When going to bag to execute double play, charge the bag hard and then have a slight hesitation or shuffle while seeing from what direction throw is coming.

6. Tag the bag with your left foot and shove off onto your right as tag is being made.

7. On a poor throw to glove side, it may be necessary at times to throw left leg to the left and then tag with right foot, throwing as right foot touches bag.

8. When possible, come across bag to get out of way of runner.

SECOND BASE

9. Use the bag as a pushing off point.

10. When starting double play, determine according to distance from bag whether a throw is necessary or if underhand shove will get the runner.

11. Draw a line in infield practice, one side of line must throw; other can shove.

12. When using the underhand shove, give it to the shortstop firmly. A stiff wrist will increase accuracy.

13. When ground ball is close enough to bag, tag bag yourself. Stay in back of bag if you can on this play.

14. Don't use the back-hand toss when feeding ball to shortstop. Hard to control.

15. Don't hide your throws. Only at one time will you turn completely around, and that is when a ball is hit real deep in hole to your left (very difficult).

16. No need to do a jump or full pivot when making double play. Catch ball, turn hips and upper part of body, bring hands and ball back, and throw.

On ball hit to your right, throw out right leg and slide along top of dirt. As ball is fielded, plant foot and throw against it.

SHORTSTOP

ON PREVIOUS PAGES WE HAVE OUTLINED THE STARTING POINTS FOR PROPER FIELDING AND THE BASIC INFIELD PROCEDURES . . . MOST ARE USED BY ALL INFIELDERS.

THE SHORTSTOP IS THE MOST IMPORTANT INFIELDER OF THEM ALL, AND HIS APPLICATION IS SOMEWHAT DIFFERENT AS HE IS THE KEY TO THE DOUBLE PLAY, DEFENSE AGAINST THE DOUBLE STEAL, CUTOFFS, ETC.

THE SHORTSTOP SHOULD:

1. Anticipate at all times what he is going to do with ball before it is hit to him.

2. Stay on top for most throws.

3. On ball hit to his right, throw out right leg and slide along top of dirt as going to ball. As ball is fielded, plant foot, and throw against it.

4. Not play too deep when double play is in order. Cut down the angle by coming in. Cheat toward bag when double play is in order.

5. Establish in own mind your weak and strong side. Cheat toward the weak side.

6. Cross over more than any other infielder because of greater area to cover.

7. Verbally keep your second baseman, third baseman, and pitcher alive.

8. Charge ball more than any other infielder.

9. Cover 2B when bunt is in order.

10. Hold runners close. Don't let them get big leads.

11. When second baseman is taking throws on double steals, advise him verbally if runner breaks from 3B toward home so that he (second baseman) can come up from the bag to make the play.

IN MAKING THE DOUBLE PLAY:

1. Do not feel every ball hit with a man on is a double-play ball. Speed of ball and where ball is hit will determine this.

2. Always get the head man. Let the second baseman execute the double play—you catch the ball.

3. Let pitcher know who is covering 2B with man on 1B.

4. Cover 2B on all balls hit back to pitcher, unless a right-handed dead pull hitter. Then second baseman takes bag.

5. Charge the bag hard. Then, slow down with a slight shuffle to see direction throw is coming from.

6. Step with left foot, then tag the bag with your right foot. This can be a tag or a drag. If ball is thrown on the outside, tag bag with right foot and shove off hard out of oncoming runner's way. If thrown on the inside, tag bag with left foot, shove off, plant right leg, and throw. When you take play by yourself, tag bag with left foot. Stay behind bag and tag the bag as you are making the throw.

7. Throw the ball low—make the runner get down.

8. Should either the shortstop or second baseman have a real weak arm, the man with the strongest arm should cover on balls hit back to the pitcher and in double-play situations.

9. Have an understanding with second baseman as to who is covering bag. Do this by hiding mouth from other team with glove. Closed mouth will mean me; open mouth will mean you.

IN MAKING THE DOUBLE PLAY, STEP WITH LEFT FOOT, THEN TAG BAG WITH RIGHT FOOT.

IF THROW IS TO THE INSIDE, TAG BAG WITH LEFT FOOT, SHOVE OFF, PLANT RIGHT LEG, AND THROW.

10. When starting double play, determine by distance from bag whether underhand shove will get the runner.

11. When using the underhand shove, give it to your second baseman firm. Stiff wrist will help accuracy.

12. Tag the bag by yourself, if possible. (Stay behind bag when making tag. As planting left foot down and making contact, release ball.)

13. Draw a line in infield practice. Establish that balls on one side of line will be shoved; other side must be thrown. When game time comes it will be fixed in your mind what to do naturally.

14. Don't hide your throws from the second baseman. Let him see the ball at all times.

15. If ball is booted, stay at bag. Act as first baseman would.

SHORTSTOP-SECOND BASEMAN—CUTOFFS AND RELAYS:

FOR BALLS IN LEFT FIELD AND LEFT-CENTER AREA, SHORTSTOP IS RELAY MAN.

FOR BALLS IN RIGHT FIELD AND RIGHT-CENTER AREA, SECOND BASEMAN IS RELAY MAN:

1. Get in position as soon as possible. Hold hands high. Make a U shape with arms and holler "hit me," "hit me." Let outfielder know where you are.

2. Take throws from the outfielder from side position and not with back facing infield. This will have your hips out of way and make it easier to get off quicker, more accurate throw. Set back foot, however. Don't throw off balance.

3. When acting as backup man, let other infielder know where to throw the ball. A loud verbal command is what is needed. Be alive for poor throw when acting as backup man.

4. When backing up other infielder, be alive for poor throw, then make play.

5. How far out you go is determined by the strength of your arm and the strength of the outfielder's arm.

6. When third baseman is acting as cutoff man, shortstop covers 3B.

7. When lining up throw from outfield, glance back to see you have positioned yourself properly for base you will be throwing to.

8. Go back on all pop flys until outfielder runs you off. Also make an effort to field all pop flys down 3B foul line until outfielder runs you off.

THIRD BASE

THE THIRD BASEMAN HAS THREE POSITIONS HE MUST TAKE:
DEEP — HALFWAY — IN

THE POSITIONS WILL BE TAKEN DEPENDING UPON THE
SCORE, OUTS, INNING, SITUATIONS, HITTER:

1. Deep position should be taken for strong right-hand hitter.

2. Deep and guard foul line when extra-base hit will allow runner to score.

3. Halfway and over for left-hand hitter.

4. Halfway in normal game situation when hitter has the ability to drag bunt.

5. Halfway for below-average hitter.

6. In when bunt is in order.

7. In for left-hand drag or push-bunt hitter.

8. In and over for left-handed pull hitter.

THE THIRD BASEMAN SHOULD:

1. Knock the ball down at all times.

2. Cut in front of shortstop and get all balls you can.

WHEN GOING TO RIGHT, PLANT FOOT AND THROW OFF IT.

3. Throw ball over the top on all balls hit right at you and to your right.

4. On balls hit to your left, at times it may be best for you to come from side.

5. Run pitchers and catchers off pop flys.

6. Go to fence and screen, then come away allowing you to be in better position to catch pop flys.

7. Know what to do with ball before it is hit to you.

8. With men on 1B and 2B and ball hit to your left, go to 2B for double play.

9. With men on 1B and 2B and ball hit to your right, tag 3B, then go to first.

10. With bases loaded and double play in order, make play easiest way. To left, go to 2B; to right, tag 3B or go home. Ball right at you: 2B, 3B, or home, whichever is easiest.

11. Act as cutoff man when man is on second and single is to left field.

12. Act as cutoff man when runner is on 3B and fly ball is to left field.

13. When acting as cutoff man, get self in position on left side of diamond between 3B dirt area and home plate.

14. Hold hands high giving outfielder a target to throw through.

15. Advise pitcher when runner is getting too big a lead off 3B.

16. Run pitcher off all topped balls that will be easier for you to field.

17. Make play on topped ball with bare hand when necessary.

18. When time allows, make small arc and come around fielding topped ball so that you are facing 1B and will not have to throw across body.

19. Start creeping slowly as pitcher is about to release ball. Getting body started will aid in getting jump on ball.

20. Do not always cross over when ball is hit to your left. Hard-hit ball won't allow this.

21. Back up throws back to pitcher after pickoff attempt when first baseman is returning ball to pitcher.

22. When going to right, plant foot and throw off it for strength and accuracy.

23. Throw from over top for strength and accuracy.

24. Encourage pitcher.

25. Be alert for squeeze, and alert pitcher for same.

26. Forget about talking to 3B coach. He will only try and distract you.

27. The topped and slow-hit balls are your toughest plays . . . practice them. IT TAKES GUTS TO PLAY THIS POSITION. YOU MUST BE A TAKE-CHARGE GUY.

28. Know how much ground the shortstop can cover.

29. Know the ability of the catcher to catch pop flys.

30. Know the fielding ability of each of your pitchers.

OUTFIELD

LIKE THE INFIELDERS, EVERY OUTFIELDER MUST SAY TO HIMSELF, "EVERY BALL HIT IS GOING TO BE HIT TO ME." PREPARE YOURSELF MENTALLY BEFORE EVERY PITCH. THAT WAY YOU WILL NEVER BE CAUGHT ON THE SHORT END.

BASIC OUTFIELD PROCEDURE TO BECOME THE COMPLETE OUTFIELDER:

1. During batting practice, shag balls in your own position.

2. Charge all ground balls during the game and in batting practice.

3. Charge all ground balls directly at infielder. Even though it may look like a sure out, get in the habit of backing up your infielders.

4. Take only one step after catching ball. Too many steps allow runners to advance, and poor throws are usually made after running with ball.

5. When throwing, at all times follow through as would pitcher. Overemphasize this when warming up and during infield practice. You will find this will strengthen your arm as well as make it more accurate.

6. Charging ball will also allow you to get more on throw.

7. Keep all throws low so that cutoff man can handle them.

8. Take one or two steps back from normal position. Then as pitcher is about to release ball start creeping, just as infielder. This will get you ready to move.

9. Keep off heels when running. Stay on balls of your feet. Running on heels will cause head to bounce and cut down speed.

10. Know score, outs.

11. Don't throw behind runner. Know what base to throw to before ball is hit.

12. Don't allow tying or winning run to get into scoring position.

13. Know weaknesses and strengths of outfielders playing alongside you.

14. Shade yourself to the side you are weak going to.

15. Back up all other outfielders.

16. Help out other outfielders verbally. Constantly tell them what to do.

17. Run the infielders off of all pop flys. The infielder will always come back until you run him off.

18. In going to ball that will be near outfield fence, go to fence first and then come away. This will prevent collisions.

19. All outfield fences are differently textured. Before game starts check out how ball will come off fence as well as how balls will react in corners.

20. Depending upon score, outs, inning, and how deep ball is hit, outfielder must decide when and when not to catch foul fly ball.

21. Know wind direction and velocity.

GETTING THE JUMP ON THE BALL AND CATCHING THE FLY BALL CORRECTLY:

1. Right-handed throwers should: On ball to right side or over your head, pivot on right foot and then cross over. On ball hit to your left side, cross over with right leg. In both cases, make certain you shove hard off of back leg when making first step.

2. Left-handed throwers should do just the opposite. Pivot on left foot, cross over with right leg when balls are hit to your left. With balls hit to your right, cross over with left leg.

To prevent collisions, go to fence first and then come away.

ALWAYS HAVE ONE LEG SLIGHTLY IN FRONT OF THE OTHER.

OUTFIELD

3. REMEMBER EVERYTHING YOU DO IN BASEBALL YOU DO OFF YOUR BACK LEG.

4. Don't trail the ball. Get yourself in position to field ball properly and make accurate, strong throws.

5. Always have one leg up in front slightly when taking outfield position.

6. On balls hit directly overhead, pivot off back leg, then cross over as necessary.

7. Try to catch all fly balls with two hands.

8. Catch balls with back of glove toward face when ball is above chest.

9. Catch balls with glove pocket facing sky when ball is below chest.

10. Be relaxed. Let ball fall into glove; don't jab at it.

11. All balls hit to the opposite field have a tendency to slice and head for foul lines. Be careful shagging the ball off of the opposite-field hitter.

12. Depending upon the wind, sun, and other physical factors, determine what position you will take in outfield. Check these things out before game starts.

13. Play as shallow as you possibly can. More base hits fall in front of outfield than they do behind.

14. When at all possible outfielders should try and catch the ball on their throwing side. This will enable them to get rid of ball much quicker.

15. Hands can be resting on knees until pitch is about ready to be made. Then bring hands off knees. As pitcher releases ball, adjust weight forward and be ready to move.

16. Call other outfielder off if you're in a better position to throw.

OUTFIELD DRILLS

1. Throw overhand and follow through as pitcher would. Slap self in back with follow-through hand.

2. Get as many ground balls as possible. If possible, shag grounders in infield, but do this as a drill not as play.

3. Pepper games are good for agility when played properly.

4. Practice the crossover even though you may not be shagging a ball.

5. Throw extended distances to strengthen arm.

6. Line up with other outfielder about 30 feet away and toss ball over each other's head. This will help develop proper way to go back on ball.

7. Practice gripping ball across seams. Get in the habit of feeling the ball correctly when making your throws.

8. CHARGE GROUND BALLS—CHARGE GROUND BALLS— CHARGE GROUND BALLS.

9. Run pitchers and all others out of your position during batting practice. The way you will learn to play it is to PLAY IT ALONE.

10. Practice catching ball off throwing foot. This saves a step, and if ball is high enough, it can be done.

11. Practice one short step when catching both ground ball and fly ball. You can't throw anyone out if you run with ball.

12. Get yourself a good big glove. But put it on your hand; don't let it lay loosely.

13. Run, run, run—an outfielder is only as good as his legs.

HITTING

BUNTING

One of the most important and probably one of the most poorly executed plays in all baseball is the bunt. More games have been lost because of someone failing to advance a man than perhaps any other reason. When bunting, remember that you are giving yourself up in order to move runners into a better scoring position. A successful bunt can also avoid the double play. A player who can bunt for a base hit is also a valuable offensive player. Let's attempt to understand the proper bunting procedure and then see to it that it is executed.

As with everything else in baseball, the starting point is the back foot. It is necessary for the bunter to turn on the ball of his back foot. I do not mean the back foot should be brought up even with the front. It is just a spin, and actually all that turns completely is the upper part of the body. This does away with completely jumping around. You can actually stay in your hitting position and get yourself ready that much quicker from there.

As you turn the upper part of your body, your knees should automatically bend slightly and your bat should come into the position covering home plate. The arms should not be extended but should be slightly bent and relaxed, bat on a 45° angle and out in front of home plate. Hold bat loosely and don't jab at the ball; let the ball come to you. As in hitting, make sure you get a good ball to bunt.

The top hand should be the contact hand and should be just about on the trademark. Use the top hand just as if you were going to catch a ball with it. In other words, top hand goes to the ball; bottom hand works as a lever and by pushing or pulling determines what side ball will be bunted on.

BUNTER SHOULD TURN ON THE BALL OF HIS BACK FOOT. IT IS NOT NECESSARY TO BRING UP THE BACK FOOT EVEN WITH THE FRONT.

HITTING

Remember:

1. Get a good ball to bunt.

2. Have bat out in front of plate and cover plate.

3. Don't stick your tail out; stay up at plate.

4. Bend knees slightly.

5. Aim for foul lines.

6. Make the RIGHT man field the ball.

7. Top hand makes the contact; bottom hand does the guiding.

Both drag and push bunting are an important part of our game and should be practiced especially by the light-hitting player who has speed. A good bunt or two per ball game can make you a much better player.

The drag and push bunter should also use the top hand as the catching hand (laying bat on ball). Practice and say to yourself, "I will catch this ball with my top hand." You will soon see how your bunts will improve. Again, aim for foul lines.

PRACTICE BUNTING AS OFTEN AS YOU CAN.

HIT AND RUN

1. This play requires a hitter who can make good contact.

2. Hitter must swing at pitch even if out of strike zone.

3. Hitter has to hit ball somewhere, but perfect hit and run is executed when ball is hit behind runner to right field. For left-handed hitter this means pulling ball.

4. Runner must glance in to home plate to locate ball about two steps after breaking for second. Don't tip play by taking unsafe lead.

5. Most important:
    For hitter—ball must be hit on the ground.
    For runner—can't be picked off base. (This is not a steal.)

BASIC HITTING FUNDAMENTALS

Perhaps the most controversial of all baseball fundamentals—as well as the most mysterious—are the basics of good hitting.

As each player is physically and mentally different, it is extremely difficult to determine what procedure is best for the individual. Below, however, are several musts in becoming a better hitter.

1. Select a bat you can handle.

2. Keep your head still.

3. Concentrate on contact.

4. Hit strikes.

5. Keep front shoulder and chin tucked in.

6. Keep your hands back.

7. Don't commit yourself too soon.

8. Forget about pulling ball—that will come.

9. Turn head so that both eyes are on pitcher. Don't look around nose.

10. Lay bat on shoulder while waiting for pitcher to get ready.

11. Don't hold bat in an erect position for any length of time. This takes strength out of your hands and arms and detracts from a free, fluid swing.

12. Learn to hit your strength. Every hitter has a strength just as every hitter has a weakness. Learn to hit your pitch. When you get it, don't let it get away.

13. Stay on the balls of your feet. Keep off heels.

14. Say to yourself, "Every pitch thrown is going to be a strike. I am going to hit every pitch." That way you will never be caught with the bat on your shoulder.

15. When stepping in to hit, make sure you have good plate coverage.

16. Don't stand in someone else's footmarks.

17. Look down and check that fat part of bat is covering home plate. Don't have handle over home plate.

18. Start the bat on every pitch to create some type of hand action and bat speed. If you like the pitch, go ahead and hit it. If you don't like the pitch, then hold up your swing.

19. Step to hit the pitch.

20. Swing down on high pitches.

21. Take a short step and stride. A long stride will only throw you off balance.

22. Don't overswing. Make contact, and the ball will go.

23. Don't be a guess hitter. Don't look for anything—hit what you see.

24. Make pitcher come to you. Don't be anxious and go after him.

25. Keep your hands back. YOU HIT WITH YOUR HANDS AND YOUR HEAD.

26. Keep your hands relaxed. As contact is made your hands will tighten.

27. When hitting to the opposite field, hit the ball on the ground and hit down on the ball.

28. Faster players should use heavier bats and should concentrate on hitting ball on the ground and making contact. Utilize speed.

29. If you're having trouble controlling bat, don't be afraid to choke. Bat control is very important.

30. Keep your tail up at home plate. Don't fall away. Keep bottom in.

31. Be aggressive with the bat. Go to home plate to hit.

32. After contact is made, follow through—don't quit on swing.

33. Hit with top hand and roll wrist.

34. Hit with hands in strike zone if swing is late.

35. WAIT — WAIT — WAIT.

SOME HITTING FAULTS
AND HOW TO CORRECT THEM

OVERSTRIDING:

1. Stride can be shortened by taking an extremely wide stance.

2. Put weight on back leg (causes hitter to keep weight back).

3. Bend knees and crouch. Shift weight to ball of back foot.

HAND HITCHES:

Getting the bat started should not be classified as a hand hitch. Most players have to start their bat in some way, and we are not concerned with this. However, if you are constantly getting hit on fist or cannot get bat back up and through in time, you may be dropping hands too much. If this is the case, you should then:

1. Move hands back rather than dropping them down.

2. Place bat on shoulder, bring up hands until they are parallel with shoulders and hit right from shoulder. Do not pick bat up—just hit off shoulder.

UPPERCUTTING:

1. Instead of vertical bat, carry a flat bat (almost parallel to the ground).

2. Lay bat on shoulder. Then, as pitcher gets ready to throw, pick bat up. This will give you freedom with hands, and the swing will have to be level as hands are right opposite shoulders.

3. Concentrate on swinging down on ball. Get the feeling of bat coming down rather than up. Actually, what you will be doing is swinging level. The bat cannot go down, or you would hit yourself on top of the feet.

4. Keep shoulders and hips level. Do not drop back shoulder to hit.

5. Practice hitting the ball on the ground.

HEAD PULLING:

1. Don't be concerned about looking to see where ball will go.

2. Watch the bat hit the ball.

3. Swing down. Think about swinging down. In taking a longer look to swing down, your head will automatically have to look at the ball longer.

4. Keep chin and shoulders tucked in. Don't be in a hurry to pull out. Your hands will take you out. Keep the head steady.

5. Forget about trying to hit the ball in the air.

6. Cut down on your swing.

7. Don't try to pull the ball.

SWEEPING THE BAT:

1. Put the bat in the fingers instead of far back in the hand.

2. Get the feeling you are hitting with your wrist only.

3. Feel the bat in your hands.

4. Relax your arms; don't try to hit with them. Roll the wrist.

BATTING DRILLS

1. If you're having trouble hitting curveball, have a pitcher who is having trouble getting curve over throw to you in batting cage.

2. Create bat speed by this drill: Have one player throw underhanded from a short distance, and have second hit ball up against screen. Do this drill at a fast pace with players switching off. This drill can be done in a small area. Make sure hitter follows through as he would any other time.

3. Create bat speed by developing strength in hands. Squeeze rubber ball or hand grips. Also do finger tip push-ups for strength.

4. If you are not blessed with natural strength, you must develop it and maintain it. A light type of weight program is helpful.

5. Hit off batting tee.

6. Swing weighted bat during winter months.

7. Practice hitting the ball to the opposite field. Hit down on the ball when doing this.

8. Take a short imaginary stride even though you may not have bat in hand.

9. To learn strike zone, extend lines out in front of home plate with your bat so that in looking at home plate it actually will look like a longer plate. This will be easier to see when in batter's box and will help you determine what pitch to hit.

10. Bring your hands through. This will automatically bring your hips through.

11. Watch the bat hit the ball in pepper games.

12. Keep head still in pepper games.

13. In batting practice as in game, don't look to the pull side of the

field. Look directly at pitcher and center field. Hands will bring ball around and you will pull automatically. Don't look to see where ball will go—keep head on target.

14. If stepping in bucket, draw a line behind you during batting practice. As you finish swing, look to see where your feet are. If they're on the other side of line, then you have not corrected your falling away.

15. Swing the bat as much as you can. Spend extra time in the batting cage. Switch off with a buddy, but hit, hit, hit.

16. Form good habits in batting practice. Give batting practice a real purpose. Have an idea. Have a plan and follow it.

17. Hit with wrist only in pepper game. Don't be concerned with stride. Get the feel of bat being just in your hands.

BASERUNNING

BASIC BASERUNNING

There are three important phases of baserunning—stealing bases, running on a batted ball from batter's box, and after becoming a base runner.

STEALING BASES:

1. The lead off base is important. Make sure there is equal distribution of weight on both feet so that you can go either way (back to the base or advance) without loss of time. The FIRST QUICK STEP is important, regardless of the way you go.

2. Break for the next base when the pitcher makes his initial move to deliver the ball. THE KNACK OF GETTING THE BREAK is the most important phase of stealing bases.
   a. Study the move of every pitcher. (This can be done when you are on the bench as well as when you are a base runner.) The pitcher may lean toward the plate, raise his front foot, or look at the runner only once before delivering the ball—any of these characteristics may be the base runner's key to advancing.

RUNNING ON BATTED BALL FROM THE BATTER'S BOX:

(If you are not one of those players adept at stealing bases, you can be a helpful and often good base runner by using the following routine. Remember, ALL PLAYERS SHOULD POSSESS SOME KNOWLEDGE OF BASERUNNING.)

1. *Run Hard* to 1B every time the ball is hit. When the ball is hit to the outfield, make the turn at 1B as if every base hit could be a two-base hit. (A slight fumble by an outfielder then gives the runner that extra base.)

2. Safeguard against making wide sweeping turns around the bases. Touch the bag with the LEFT foot whenever possible, but if you cannot hit the bag with the left foot, do not break stride to do so. Get in the baseline (straight line between each base, or as close to a straight line as possible) after passing each base.

3. Know which of the opposing outfielders can throw well.

4. Know where your opponents play for you.

5. Know whether outfielder handling the batted ball is right- or left-handed. If the ball is handled on the off side (usually the glove hand), the outfielder will take a little more time to throw the ball. This makes it possible for the runner to gain a step or more on the batted ball.

ALWAYS RUN WITH YOUR HEAD UP—YOU CAN FOLLOW THE PLAY BETTER. IF THE BALL IS HIT OUT OF YOUR VISION OR BEHIND YOU (TO RIGHT-FIELD CORNER FOR POSSIBLE TRIPLE), LOOK AT THE THIRD-BASE COACH FOR THE SIGNAL TO STOP OR CONTINUE TO THIRD BASE.

AFTER YOU BECOME A BASE RUNNER:

1. Always keep in mind the number of outs.

2. Find out who has the ball. (If the pitcher is on the mound, he must have possession of the ball; otherwise it is a balk.)

3. Look for a possible sign (hit and run or steal).

4. Get a reasonable, comfortable lead. (Don't lean toward 2B or appear anxious to go if the hit-and-run play is on. This may tip off the play to an observing opponent.)

5. Follow the ball from the pitcher's hand to the batter, and either advance as the ball comes in contact with the bat, or, if the ball is not hit, GO BACK TO YOUR BASE AS QUICKLY AS POSSIBLE to safeguard against being caught on a possible pickoff play.

6. If advancing on a hit-and-run play, glance over your left shoulder to see where the ball is hit—if you cannot FIND the ball, look at your coaches for a signal where to go and what to do. (Do not let opposing fielder decoy you into believing the ball is hit on the ground if it is hit in the air.)

7. To break up the double play (at 2B): Some infielders find it difficult to get out of the baseline when handling the ball at 2B on the possible double play. The runner is entitled to the baseline. Always slide into 2B on this play. This makes it difficult for the man handling the ball to get it away to 1B in time to complete the play.

REMINDERS:

1. Where is the ball?

2. How many are out?

3. Look for a possible sign.

4. Don't talk to the opposing infielders. Often this is done to distract your attention and may cost you a base you otherwise might have advanced.

5. Always run with your head up.

BASERUNNING RULES

BE AGGRESSIVE ON THE BASES. TAG EACH BASE WITH ONE THING IN MIND AND THAT IS GETTING TO THE NEXT ONE. REMEMBER THE SHORTEST DISTANCE BETWEEN TWO PLACES IS A STRAIGHT LINE.

YOU CAN'T BE AGGRESSIVE WHEN YOU ARE CONFUSED ON THE BASES, SO KNOW WHAT YOU ARE DOING.

WHEN RUNNING THE BASES:

1. Go in a straight line when running to 1B.

2. Don't run on infield grass.

3. Run every ball out. Infielders will make errors—there is no such thing as a sure out.

4. Run hard at all times.

5. When attempting to beat out a ground ball or bunt, run past the bag—don't hold up.

6. Don't look at ball hit to infield. Look at 1B and run to it.

7. Shove hard off back foot, then take first step with back leg. A good quick getaway may be the difference between being safe or out.

8. Don't break stride to touch bases.

9. After getting a base hit, have only one thing in mind—and that is going to 2B or 3B. Take a slight turn out, tag the bag with either foot, and then say in your mind, "I know I am going to second base." There is no doubt in your mind. After following the ball and seeing the outfielder come up with it cleanly, you then can return to the 1B bag. However, should the ball be fumbled for just a moment, then 2B is not an impossibility. The same thing ap-

plies going into 2B or 3B. You tag the bag with one thing in mind, and that is going to the next base.

10. Wide turns lengthen the distance between bases. Keep the turns short. There is no need to make the wide turn if you think about what you are doing as you approach the bag. NO WIDE SWEEPS.

11. Base runners must always look to see where outfielders are playing. If the ball is hit so that outfielder is out of position, the runner will have the advantage when taking the extra base because he will know the outfielder will have a more difficult time positioning himself for fielding and throwing the ball.

12. When you are base runner with the hit and run or run and hit, you should glance back and have some idea where the ball has been hit.

13. Don't run with your head down; be alert.

14. As a base runner, make certain you know and GET ALL SIGNS.

15. TOUCH THE BASES.

16. Tag the bases on the front end, which is nearest the pitcher's mound.

17. Know the number of outs.

18. An aggressive base runner will make both infielders and outfielders mishandle balls.

19. Know the score.

20. You should have only one thing in mind when on base—SCORE.

21. Watch infield to determine strengths of catcher's, outfielders', and infielders' arms.

LEADS

GO-GO BASERUNNING IS EXCITING TO THE FAN AS WELL AS SATISFYING AND FUN FOR THE PLAYER. WHEN YOU BECOME A BASE RUNNER THINK ABOUT CREATING AN ATMOSPHERE OF EXCITEMENT.

You must want to steal bases.
You must want to score runs.
You must want to take the extra bases.
You must want to run.

WHEN LEADING OFF 1B:

1. Two and one-half steps is a normal safe lead off 1B.

2. Your hands should be off knees.

3. No jumping back and forth.

4. Have arms slightly raised.

5. You can get your 2½ steps in two ways: slight shuffling lead, or by just walking off.

6. Stay on the bag until pitcher has taken his place on the rubber.

7. Find out who has ball before you get off base.

8. When taking a walking lead, take as much as you can until pitcher makes you stop. This is even more important when stealing a base. If you are taking a walking lead and he does not make you stop, then keep on going but be careful not to be caught leaning. Walk nonchalantly off and be inconspicuous.

9. At times, when wanting to test a pitcher's move, get off the base with the idea of definitely going back into 1B. Tease him but be careful.

10. Study the pitcher's move before becoming a base runner.

11. After taking your walking lead or shuffling lead, and deciding you now must make your next move (either to steal a base or advance as a runner), the crossover step should be your next move.

12. Know the strength of the catcher's arm.

13. Look at the infielders to see how they are shading the hitter.

14. Don't give steal away by bobbing your head or waving your arms.

15. Know the strength of outfielders' arms.

16. Check to see where outfielders are playing.

17. As a runner on 1B when there is also a man on 2B, at all times be alive for the double steal. Third base should never be stolen without man on first advancing to second. When this situation is possible, always know the man on 2B is going to 3B. You then will never be caught looking.

18. You need not be an extremely fast runner to steal bases, although it is helpful. Studying the pitcher's delivery and moves, plus your own aggressiveness, can make many ordinary runners base stealers.

WHEN GETTING THE LEAD OFF SECOND BASE:

THE LEAD OFF SECOND BASE IS VERY IMPORTANT—THE RUNNER IS NOW HALFWAY HOME. ALERTNESS AND AGGRESSIVENESS STILL REMAIN THE IMPORTANT FACTORS.

1. Get as much of a lead as the second baseman, shortstop, and pitcher will allow you to take.

2. Listen to your 3B coach. He will advise you of the shortstop's and second baseman's positions. It is up to you as a runner to watch the pitcher.

3. As the pitcher is throwing home, make certain you are on the balls of your feet and going forward. Don't be caught leaning back.

MAJOR LEAGUE BASEBALL MANUAL

4. As a base runner on 2B, make certain that all ground balls hit to your right go through the infielder before you advance.

5. On ground balls hit to your left, you should advance to 3B.

6. A pitcher will sometimes be lax in holding the runner on 2B. Should this be the case, and depending upon the score, outs, inning, and runner, 3B is sometimes an easy base to steal.

7. Do not try to advance when ball is hit back to the pitcher.

WHEN GETTING LEAD OFF THIRD BASE:

1. Always stay in foul territory (not too far off line, however).

2. Slow windup or fast windup by the pitcher will determine when you will start making your move toward home plate.

3. As the pitcher starts his windup, start walking toward home plate. Just keep walking—always have yourself going toward home plate. Go as far as you can, stop and watch the pitch be delivered, then return to the base.

4. Never be caught running back and forth. You may be caught leaning in the wrong direction.

5. When you are walking in, be alive for passed balls and wild pitches.

6. After you've moved in and seen the catcher receive the ball, turn to the left and return to base.

7. As a runner on 3B, there may be a time when you can score when a ground ball does not get through the infield. This can be done by looking to see where the infielders have positioned themselves. If they have to move in any difficult direction, it will be tough for them to regain position and make proper throw to home plate.

TAGGING UP TO ADVANCE TO HOME OR TO OTHER BASES:

1. Don't start from behind the bag and then try to time the outfielder's catch.

2. Don't have foot on bag with a sprinter's starting stance (finger tips on ground, front foot forward, and bent leg).

3. Do not listen for the coach to give word signal. You yourself must determine when to go.

4. Runner should start from upright position, knees slightly bent, one foot on bag (whichever foot runner feels strongest for him to shove off with). Watch flight of the ball, and when ball is caught, shove hard and head for next base.

5. Run hard at all times to home plate; don't slow up at any time. Hit it hard.

STEALING TECHNIQUES

ONE WHO DOESN'T HAVE LARCENY IN HIS BLOOD CANNOT BE A GOOD BASE STEALER.

BASE RUNNERS MUST BE:

Aggressive
Daring
Courageous
Confident
Able to concentrate
Smart

Most people feel speed is the only thing a stealer has to have. Speed alone is NOT the answer. Speed in connection with study and concentration helps form a "picture" of the art of successful stealing. Concentration is important. Add the ingredients of PRACTICE, PRACTICE, PRACTICE, and experimentation, and there are fewer pieces missing.

BASES ARE STOLEN BEFORE THE GAME:

CATCHER: Watch every throw during infield practice. Time with stopwatch if possible. Ask yourself these questions:

1. Has he a good arm?

2. Does he throw accurately?

3. Does he have a quick release?

4. Did the starting catcher throw infield? If he didn't, perhaps his arm is sore. Watch him return throws to the pitcher and to 2B at the start of an inning.

5. Has the catcher taken any foul balls off the hand, arm, or fingers during the game?

PITCHER: Watch every starting pitcher warm up before a game and ask yourself these questions:

RIGHT-HAND PITCHERS

1. Is his delivery slow?

2. Is his delivery fast?

3. Is his delivery long or sweeping?

4. Have we timed the pitcher with men on base?

5. From a balk position, is he slow in his movement (high kick, etc.)?

6. Does the pitcher always deliver on the same count?

LEFT-HAND PITCHERS

1. Does he give any head fake from a balk position? If he does, he probably will in the game.

2. Does he continue to make a big kick with runner on 2B?

PITCHERS: Watch the pitcher during the game as well as before. Every thief on the bench should know EARLY IN THE GAME when the first runner gets to 1B:

1. What kind of move does he have?

2. Does he have a pattern of throwing home and to 1B?

3. Does he throw often to 1B, or not at all?

4. Is he wild to the plate? He may be wild to 1B.

5. Does he give away when he's going to home or to 1B?

6. Does he bounce his curve a lot?

INFIELDERS (SECOND BASEMAN AND SHORTSTOP): You should always watch the second baseman and shortstop take infield practice and ask yourself:

1. Do they take throws in front of the bag?

2. Are they quick?

3. Are their hands good in infield practice?

4. Are they shy when other thieves go into 2B?

5. Do they "cheat" for the double play or steal, or is the covering in-fielder far from 2B?

6. Between pitches, do they relax and leave 2B unguarded?

FIRST BASEMAN: You should know how good a fielder the first baseman is and:

1. Is he right- or left-handed? (Left-handers can tag you quicker.)

2. Is he big and slow?

3. Are his hands good?

4. Does he tag quickly?

5. Does he reach for the ball?

6. Carefully watching the first baseman in infield practice and as he attempts to tag your teammates will give you a clue.

STEALING THIRD BASE: Every runner must know two basics about stealing 3B:

1. You must be moving on the delivery.

2. You steal on the pitcher.

STEALING 3B IS A "SURPRISE STEAL." You carefully analyze the pitcher for:

1. Does his team have pickoff plays? Can he execute the play?

2. How alert is he?

3. Does he see exactly where you are?

4. How much attention does he give you? Is he fully concentrating on the hitter?

5. Is the infielder nearest 2B aggressive or not? Does he fake you back, and is he close or not?

6. It is best at first to be conservative at 2B so you don't tip your hand.

SUMMATION:

To excel in becoming a professional thief, you must take great pride in the fact that you have excelled. Study of your competition should include keeping a book on all pitchers you face, remembering to note if it is easy to get a jump on them, if they have exceptional pickoff moves, if they can be easily upset by a thief's agitating at 1B. Write down how well the catchers throw, and note anything at all that will help you steal your quota of bases.

GOOD LUCK!

Remember—all players can be good base runners, but only players with speed and knowledge can be good BASE-BURNING BREWERS.

THE DOUBLE STEAL

AS A BASE RUNNER YOU SHOULD WANT TO STEAL BASES. ONE WAY YOU CAN DO THIS IS TO STEAL NOT ONLY SECOND OR THIRD BASE BY THEMSELVES, BUT ALSO TO BE A PART OF THE DOUBLE STEAL.

1. The runner on 1B has one thing in mind and that is going into 2B as hard as he can. Then upon seeing the infielder laying back to make the tag on him, he must hold up and get in a rundown so that the man on 3B will then be allowed to score. Should the infielder not lay back but come up in front of the bag to make the throw for the man going home, then, of course, the runner should continue on into 2B.

2. The runner on 3B, when knowing the double steal is in order, will walk directly on the 3B foul line. Since he is walking on the foul line and in line with 3B bag, catcher will have a difficult time determining how big a lead he has. The runner will come to a stop when he has gotten an extended safe lead. He will watch the pitcher throw the ball to home plate. The runner on 1B will then break for 2B. The runner on 3B, upon seeing the catcher's throw to 2B go over pitcher's head, will then head for home.

    Be careful of return throw to pitcher as well as fake throw to 2B followed by throw to 3B. MAKE CERTAIN YOU SEE THROW GO OVER PITCHER'S HEAD.

SLIDING

THERE ARE MANY APPROACHES TO THE PROPER METHOD OF SLIDING. THE BEST APPROACH TO SLIDING IS THE SIMPLEST AND FASTEST WAY TO THE BAG. THEREFORE, WE WILL FIRST TEACH THE BENT-LEG, STRAIGHT-IN SLIDE. THE MORE ADEPT PLAYER CAN VARY THIS WITH HOOK SLIDES, ETC.

THE BENT-LEG SLIDE:

1. To learn the bent-leg slide: remove your spikes.

2. Go to the outfield grass with practice pants or coveralls on.

3. Line up and work as a group.

4. All players will actually be doing is sitting down when first starting (nature will tuck leg under you).

5. Use a loose bag to slide into.

6. Start first at a short distance, then increase as confidence is gained.

7. Make slide in half-sitting position on calf of bottom leg.

8. You can bend bottom leg or both legs when first starting.

9. Ride bottom leg on bent position.

10. Be relaxed, don't fight it. A slide is a glide.

11. Throw your head back slightly as you start slide.

12. Throw your arms up for balance.

13. As a rule you will slide on one side better than another. Find out what is best side for you. This will be your master side. Slide on it.

14. Slide straight into bag. Should you have to avoid tag, then slide on one side of the bag or the other and use your hand to touch base. This can also be done when avoiding a tag at home plate.

15. Start your slide about 6 or 8 feet from bag. BE CAREFUL NEVER TO SLIDE TOO LATE.

16. ONCE YOU HAVE DECIDED TO SLIDE, NEVER CHANGE YOUR MIND. IT DOESN'T HURT TO ALWAYS SLIDE, BUT YOU CAN GET HURT BY NOT SLIDING.

To do a pop-up slide, keep top leg free

BASERUNNING

17. To do a pop-up slide (this will help runner continue on to next base), lift yourself slightly as you slide along with good speed (good speed is always a factor in a proper slide). Raise yourself up as you gain momentum. Keep top leg free. Rise on your bottom leg and continue on.

18. When doing bent-leg slide and being tagged out, don't be afraid to use top leg and foot to jar baseball out of the infielder's glove.

19. Protect your leg and bottom by using sliding pads. Protect your knees by using knee pad or pulling up baseball socks.

AND RISE ON YOUR BOTTOM LEG.

THE HOOK SLIDE:

1. Used for sliding away from tag.

2. Forces fielder to make longer tag.

3. Can be used on either side of bag. Ordinarily you hook to fielder's bare-hand side, but if he is receiving throw on hand side, slide to glove side.

4. The hook automatically makes you a smaller target as only your foot is open for tag.

DEFENSIVE ASSIGNMENTS

SITUATION 1

SINGLE TO LEFT FIELD

No one on base.

PITCHER: Move to a position halfway between mound and 2B.

CATCHER: Follow runner down to 1B.

FIRST BASEMAN: Make sure the runner tags the base in making the turn, then cover 1B.

SHORTSTOP: Act as cutoff man in short left field.

SECOND BASEMAN: Cover 2B.

THIRD BASEMAN: Protect 3B area.

OUTFIELDERS: Center fielder—back up left fielder. Right fielder—move in toward 1B area.

Note possible switch of shortstop and third baseman on ground single.

DEFENSIVE ASSIGNMENTS

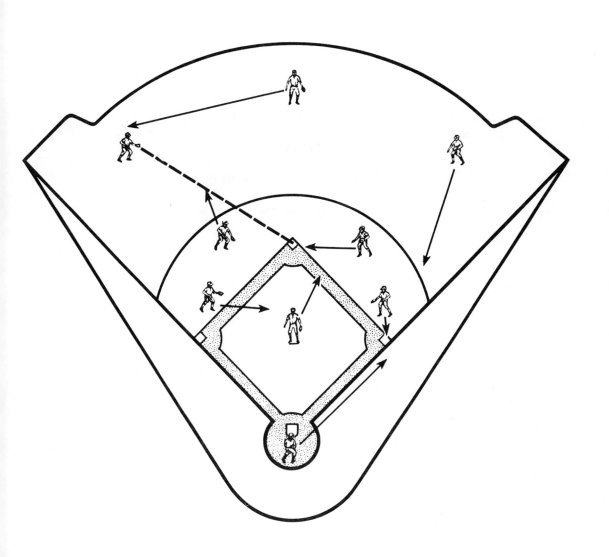

SITUATION 1

SITUATION 2

SINGLE TO LEFT FIELD

Man on 1B.

PITCHER: Back up 3B.

CATCHER: Protect home-plate area.

FIRST BASEMAN: Cover 1B.

SECOND BASEMAN: Cover 2B.

SHORTSTOP: Move into a position to be the cutoff man on the throw to 3B.

THIRD BASEMAN: Cover 3B.

CENTER FIELDER: Back up left fielder.

RIGHT FIELDER: Move in toward infield area.

DEFENSIVE ASSIGNMENTS

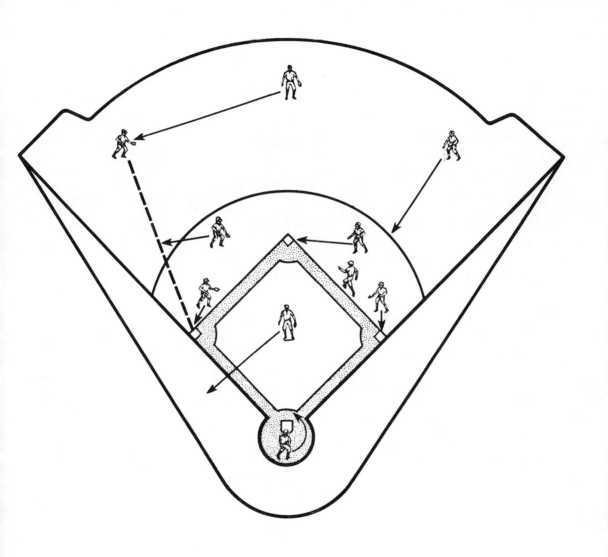

SITUATION 2

SITUATION 3

SINGLE TO LEFT FIELD

Man on 2B, or
Men on 1B and 2B, or
Bases loaded.

PITCHER: Back up home plate.

CATCHER: Cover home plate.

FIRST BASEMAN: Cover 1B.

SECOND BASEMAN: Cover 2B.

SHORTSTOP: Cover 3B.

THIRD BASEMAN: Be the cutoff man.

CENTER FIELDER: Back up left fielder.

RIGHT FIELDER: Move in toward 2B area.

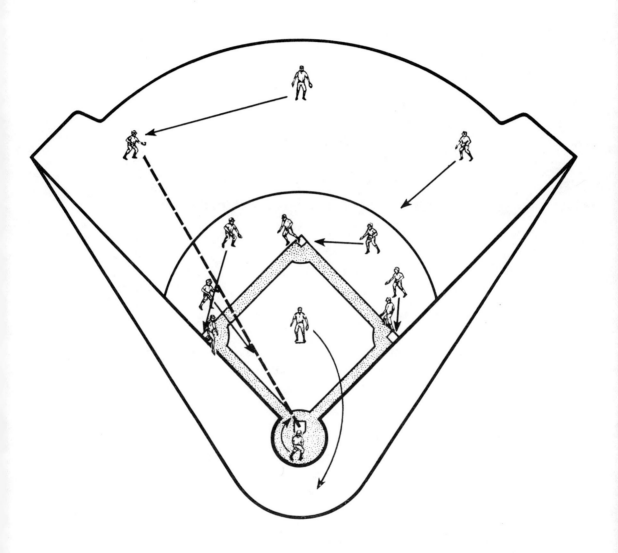

SITUATION 3

SITUATION 4

SINGLE TO LEFT FIELD
BETWEEN SHORTSTOP AND THIRD BASEMAN

Man on 2B, or

Men on 2B and 3B.

PITCHER: Back up home plate.

CATCHER: Cover home plate.

FIRST BASEMAN: Cutoff man! Take a position about 45 feet from home plate in line with left fielder and home plate.

SECOND BASEMAN: Cover 2B.

SHORTSTOP: May have to cover 3B if third baseman cannot recover.

THIRD BASEMAN: Cover 3B if possible.

LEFT FIELDER: Make low throw to the plate.

CENTER FIELDER: Back up left fielder.

RIGHT FIELDER: Come in quickly to try and cover 1B.

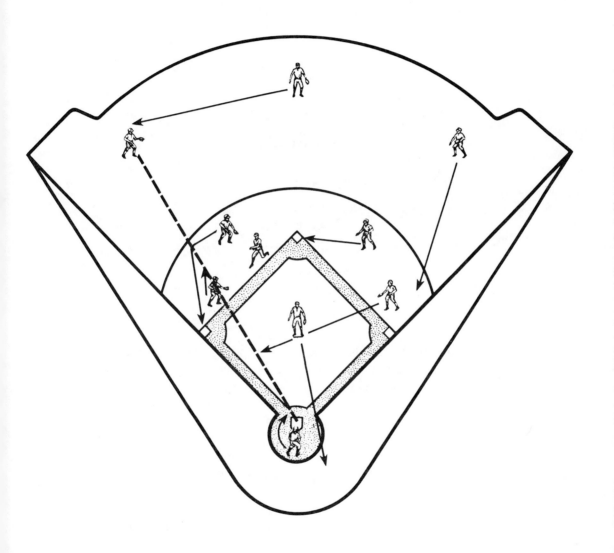

SITUATION 4

SITUATION 5

SINGLE TO LEFT FIELD

Judgment Play

Man on 2B

Hitter is the tying run.

PITCHER: Move off mound to back up home plate in case the left fielder makes the throw home.

CATCHER: Cover home plate.

FIRST BASEMAN: Cover 1B.

SECOND BASEMAN: Cover 2B.

SHORTSTOP: Cutoff position.

THIRD BASEMAN: Move into position to be cutoff man in case the left fielder throws home.

LEFT FIELDER: Make low throw to 2B to keep batter from advancing into scoring position.

CENTER FIELDER: Back up left fielder.

RIGHT FIELDER: Move into position to help back up 2B.

Never let the tying run get into scoring position at 2B by making a foolish throw to the plate.

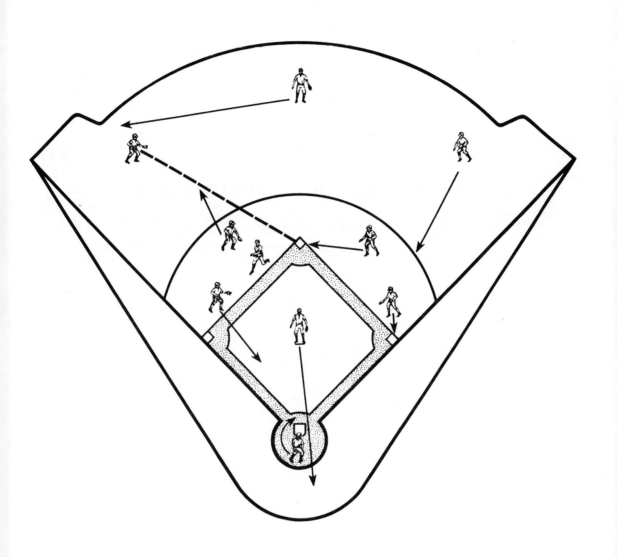

SITUATION 5

SITUATION 6

DOUBLE, POSSIBLE TRIPLE, TO LEFT CENTER

No one on base, or

Man on 3B or 2B, or

Men on 3B and 2B.

PITCHER: Back up 3B in line with throw.

CATCHER: Protect home plate.

FIRST BASEMAN: Trail the runner to 2B, cover the bag, ready for a play if runner rounds base too far.

SECOND BASEMAN: Trail about 30 feet behind shortstop in line with 3B.

SHORTSTOP: Go to a spot in left center to become relay man.

THIRD BASEMAN: Cover 3B; stand on left side of base.

CENTER FIELDER: Back up the left fielder.

RIGHT FIELDER: Move in toward 2B.

DEFENSIVE ASSIGNMENTS

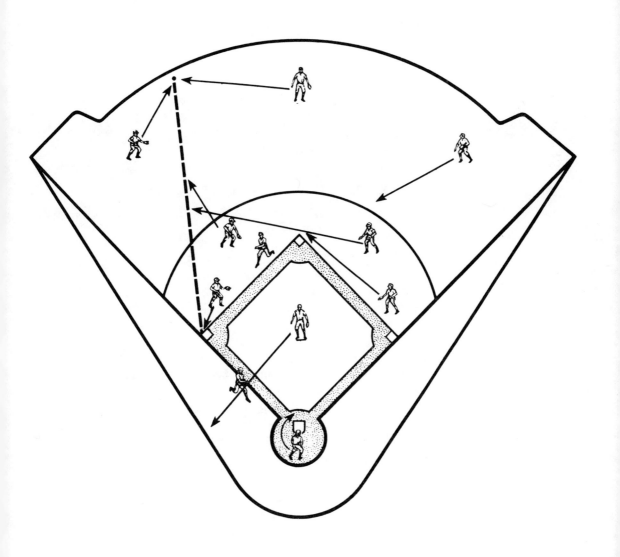

SITUATION 6

SITUATION 7

DOUBLE, POSSIBLE TRIPLE, TO LEFT CENTER

Man on 1B, or

Men on 1B and 2B, or

Bases loaded.

PITCHER: Go halfway between home and 3B and then back up the base where throw is going.

CATCHER: Protect home plate.

FIRST BASEMAN: Be the cutoff man.

SECOND BASEMAN: Trail about 30 feet behind shortstop in line with 3B.

SHORTSTOP: Go to a spot in left center to become relay man.

THIRD BASEMAN: Cover 3B; stand on left side of base.

CENTER FIELDER: Back up the left fielder.

RIGHT FIELDER: Move in to cover 2B.

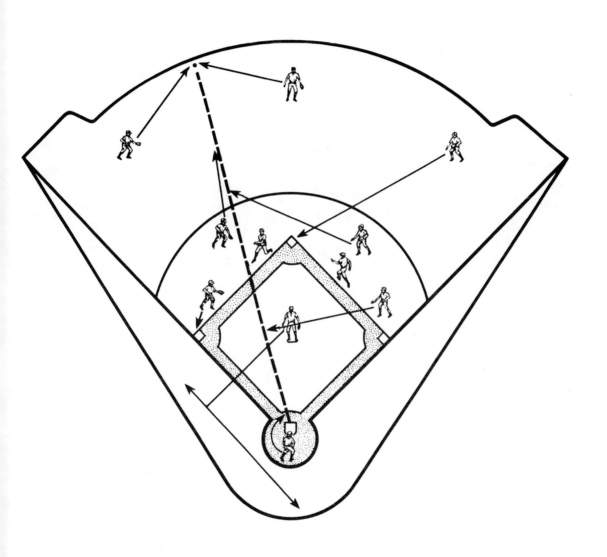

SITUATION 7

SITUATION 8

DOUBLE, POSSIBLE TRIPLE,
DOWN LEFT-FIELD FOUL LINE

Man on 1B.

PITCHER: Back up home plate.

CATCHER: Cover home plate.

FIRST BASEMAN: Become the cutoff man.

SECOND BASEMAN: Become trailer behind the shortstop.

SHORTSTOP: Relay man!

THIRD BASEMAN: Cover 3B.

CENTER FIELDER: Back up left fielder.

RIGHT FIELDER: Cover 2B.

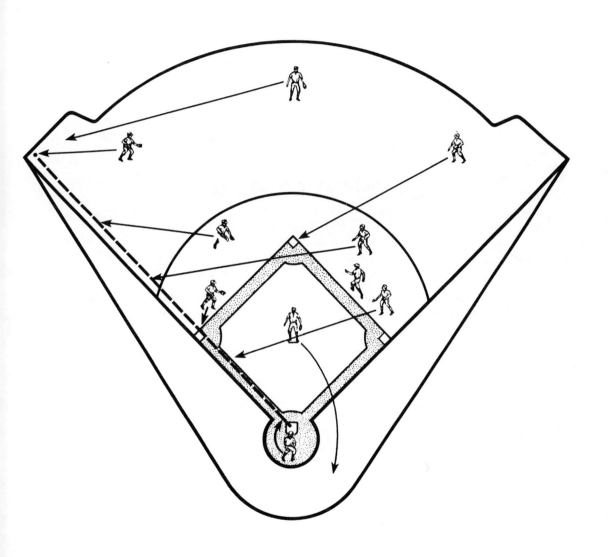

SITUATION 8

SITUATION 9

SINGLE TO CENTER FIELD

No one on base.

PITCHER: Move to a position half-way between mound and 2B.

CATCHER: Protect home-plate area.

FIRST BASEMAN: Make sure the runner tags the base in making the turn, then cover 1B.

SHORTSTOP: Cover 2B or take relay throw from center fielder.

SECOND BASEMAN: Cover 2B or take relay throw from center fielder.

THIRD BASEMAN: Protect 3B area.

OUTFIELDERS: Left and right fielders back up center fielder.

DEFENSIVE ASSIGNMENTS

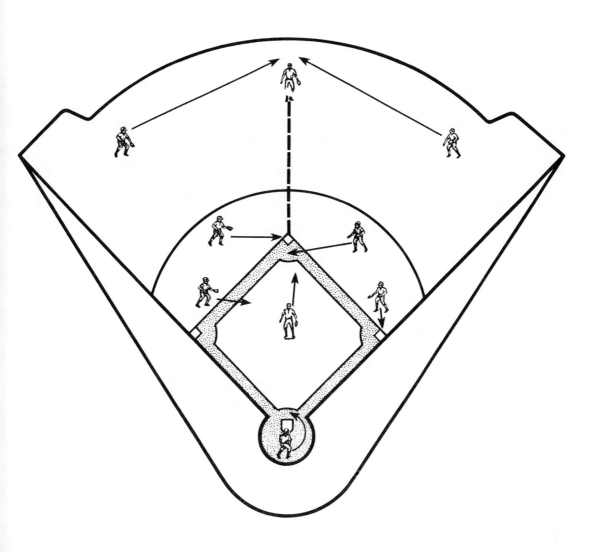

SITUATION 9

SITUATION 10

SINGLE TO CENTER FIELD

Man on 1B.

PITCHER: Back up 3B.

CATCHER: Protect home-plate area.

FIRST BASEMAN: Cover 1B.

SECOND BASEMAN: Cover 2B.

SHORTSTOP: Be cutoff man on throw from center field to 3B.

THIRD BASEMAN: Cover 3B.

LEFT AND RIGHT FIELDERS: Back up center fielder.

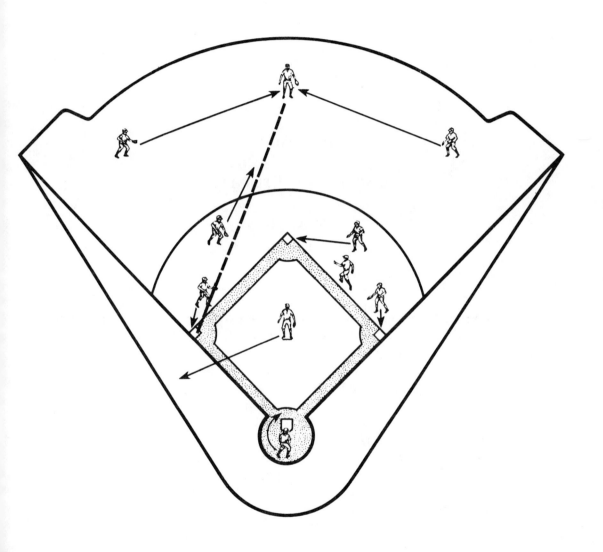

SITUATION 10

SITUATION 11

SINGLE TO CENTER FIELD

Man on 2B, or

Men on 2B and 3B.

PITCHER: Back up home plate.

CATCHER: Cover home plate.

FIRST BASEMAN: Be the cutoff man.

SECOND BASEMAN: Go after ball. If possible, return to cover 1B.

SHORTSTOP: Go after ball. Then cover 2B.

THIRD BASEMAN: Cover 3B.

LEFT FIELDER: Back up center fielder.

RIGHT FIELDER: Back up center fielder.

DEFENSIVE ASSIGNMENTS

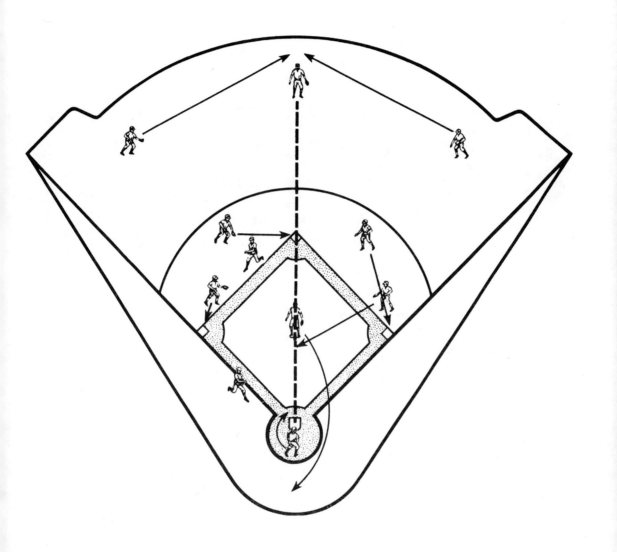

SITUATION 11

151

SITUATION 12

SINGLE TO CENTER FIELD

Men on 1B and 2B, or

Men on 1B, 2B, and 3B.

PITCHER: Go halfway between home and 3B, and then back up the base where the throw is going.

CATCHER: Cover home plate.

FIRST BASEMAN: Move into a spot 45 feet from home plate in line with the throw, to be cutoff man. If throw goes to 3B, hustle back to 1B to cover that base.

SECOND BASEMAN: Cover 2B.

SHORTSTOP: Be the cutoff man for a possible throw to 3B.

THIRD BASEMAN: Cover 3B.

LEFT FIELDER: Back up center fielder.

RIGHT FIELDER: Back up center fielder.

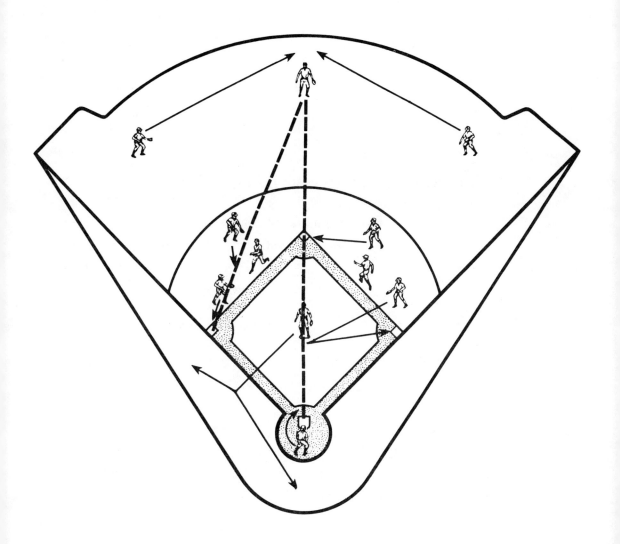

SITUATION 12

SITUATION 13

FLY BALL TO CENTER FIELD OR RIGHT FIELD

Runners on 1B and 3B, or

Bases loaded.

PITCHER: Back up home plate.

CATCHER: Cover home plate.

FIRST BASEMAN: Be the cutoff man.

SECOND BASEMAN: Cover 1B.

SHORTSTOP: Cover 2B.

THIRD BASEMAN: Cover 3B.

LEFT FIELDER: Move toward fly ball.

RIGHT FIELDER: Move toward fly ball.

DEFENSIVE ASSIGNMENTS

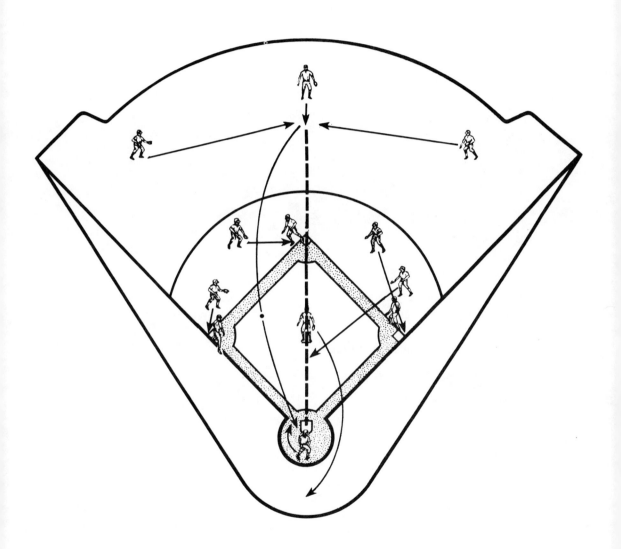

SITUATION 13

SITUATION 14

SINGLE TO RIGHT FIELD

No one on base.

PITCHER: Move to a position half-way between mound and 2B.

CATCHER: Protect home-plate area.

FIRST BASEMAN: Make sure the runner tags the base in making the turn, then cover 1B.

SHORTSTOP: Cover 2B.

SECOND BASEMAN: Go out to take throw from right fielder.

THIRD BASEMAN: Protect 3B area.

OUTFIELDERS: Center fielder back up right fielder. Left fielder move in toward 3B.

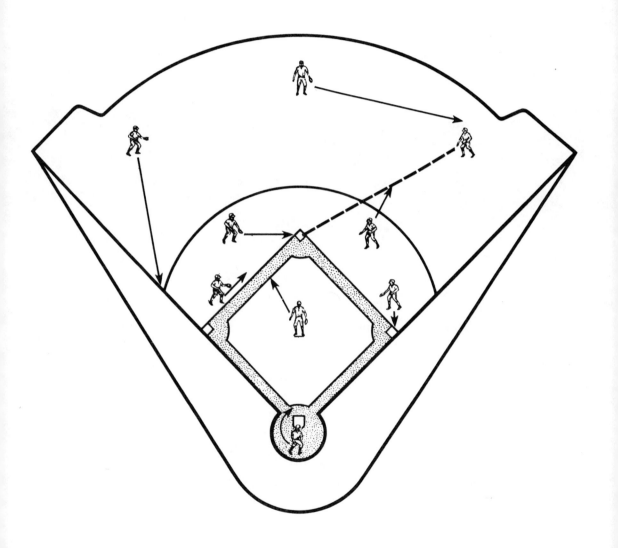

SITUATION 14

SITUATION 15

SINGLE TO RIGHT FIELD

Man on 1B, or

Men on 3B and 1B.

PITCHER: Back up 3B in line with throw.

CATCHER: Protect home plate.

FIRST BASEMAN: Cover 1B. Make sure runner tags 1B.

SECOND BASEMAN: Cover 2B. Make sure runner tags 2B.

SHORTSTOP: Station yourself about 45 feet from 3B, on a direct line from 3B to the outfielder fielding the ball.

THIRD BASEMAN: Cover 3B.

LEFT FIELDER: Move in toward 3B.

CENTER FIELDER: Back up right fielder.

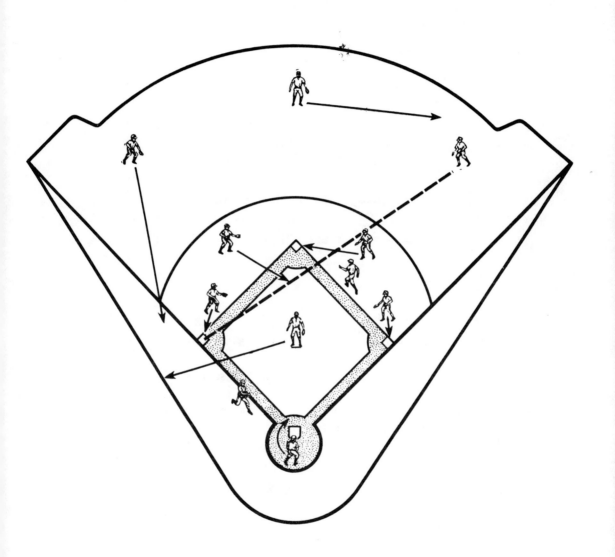

SITUATION 15

SITUATION 16

SINGLE TO RIGHT FIELD

Man on 2B, or

Men on 2B and 3B.

PITCHER: Back up home plate.

CATCHER: Cover home plate.

FIRST BASEMAN: Take position about 45 feet from home plate to become cutoff man.

SECOND BASEMAN: Cover 1B.

SHORTSTOP: Cover 2B.

THIRD BASEMAN: Cover 3B.

LEFT FIELDER: Move in toward 2B.

CENTER FIELDER: Back up right fielder.

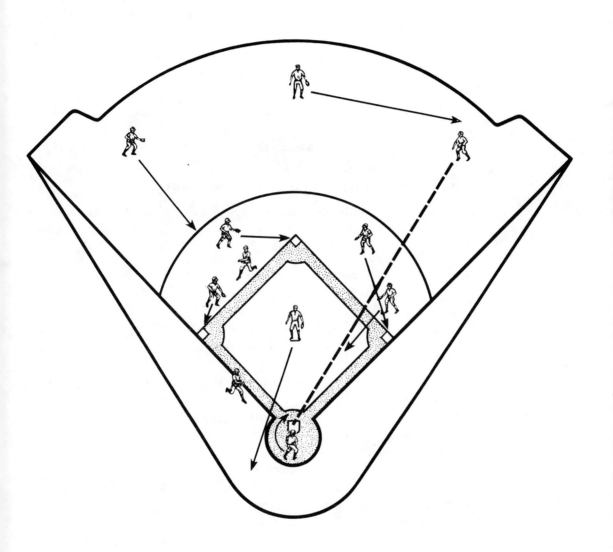

SITUATION 16

SITUATION 17

SINGLE TO RIGHT FIELD BETWEEN FIRST AND SECOND BASEMEN

Man on 2B, or

Men on 2B and 3B.

PITCHER: Start to cover 1B, then back up home plate.

CATCHER: Cover home plate.

FIRST BASEMAN: After attempting to field ball, return to cutoff position.

SECOND BASEMAN: After attempting to field ball, continue to cover 1B.

SHORTSTOP: Cover 2B.

THIRD BASEMAN: Cover 3B.

LEFT FIELDER: Move into area behind 3B.

CENTER FIELDER: Back up right fielder, move in toward 2B after ball is fielded.

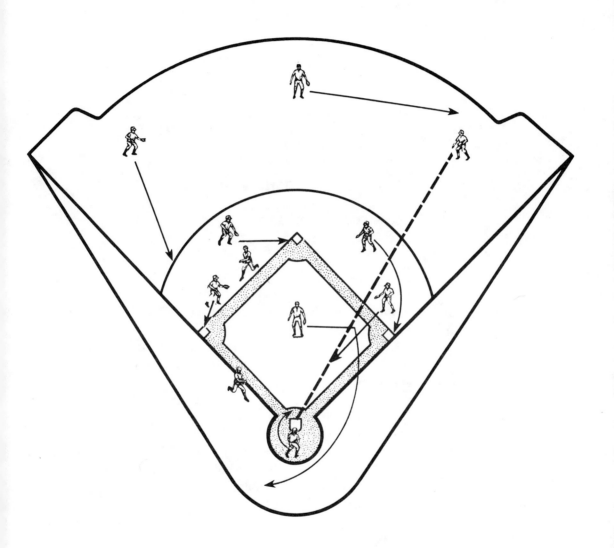

SITUATION 17

SITUATION 18

SINGLE TO RIGHT FIELD

Men on 1B and 2B, or

Men on 1B, 2B, and 3B.*

PITCHER: Go halfway between 3B and home to see where the throw goes.

CATCHER: Cover home plate.

FIRST BASEMAN: Become a cutoff man in case the throw is made to the plate. If throw goes to 3B, cover 1B.

SECOND BASEMAN: Cover 2B.

SHORTSTOP: Cutoff man for the throw to 3B.

THIRD BASEMAN: Cover 3B.

LEFT FIELDER: Move to a point near the line and back up 3B.

CENTER FIELDER: Back up right fielder.

RIGHT FIELDER: Make a low throw to the shortstop to keep the tying or winning run from going to 3B.

* ALWAYS keep tying or winning run from going to 3B with less than two out. Give opposing team two runs to keep the tying run at 2B in this situation. NEVER make a foolish throw to the plate.

DEFENSIVE ASSIGNMENTS

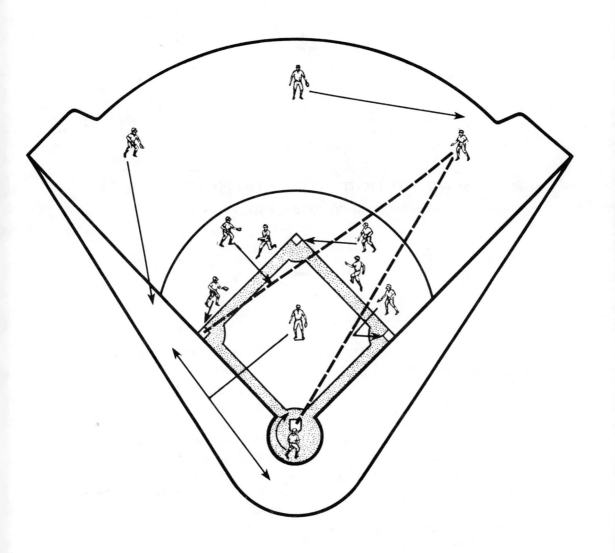

SITUATION 18

SITUATION 19

SINGLE TO RIGHT FIELD BETWEEN FIRST AND SECOND BASEMEN

Men on 1B and 2B, or

Bases loaded.

PITCHER: Start to cover 1B, and when ball gets through, back up necessary base.

CATCHER: Cover home plate.

FIRST BASEMAN: When you can't field the ball, return to cutoff position.

SECOND BASEMAN: When you can't field the ball, continue on to cover 1B.

SHORTSTOP: Cutoff man for a possible throw to 3B.

THIRD BASEMAN: Cover 3B.

LEFT FIELDER: Move into area behind 3B to help backup.

CENTER FIELDER: Back up the right fielder.

DEFENSIVE ASSIGNMENTS

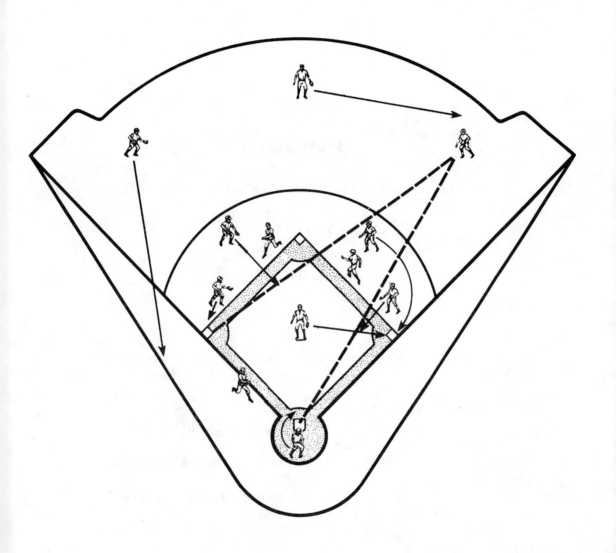

SITUATION 19

SITUATION 20

DOUBLE, POSSIBLE TRIPLE, TO RIGHT CENTER FIELD

No one on base, or

Man on 3B or 2B, or

Men on 3B and 2B.

PITCHER: Back up 3B. Get as deep as possible.

CATCHER: Protect home plate.

FIRST BASEMAN: Trail the runner to 2B; cover the bag, ready for a play at that base.

SECOND BASEMAN: Go to spot in center field, in line with 3B, to become relay man.

SHORTSTOP: Trail about 30 feet behind second baseman, in line with 3B.

THIRD BASEMAN: Cover 3B.

LEFT FIELDER: Move in toward 3B.

RIGHT FIELDER: Back up center fielder.

DEFENSIVE ASSIGNMENTS

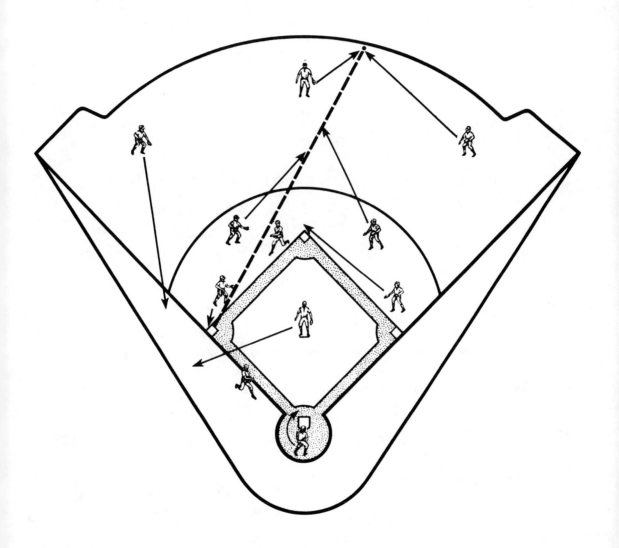

SITUATION 20

SITUATION 21

DOUBLE, POSSIBLE TRIPLE, TO RIGHT CENTER FIELD

Man on 1B, or

Men on 1B and 2B, or

Bases loaded.

PITCHER: Go halfway between 3B and the plate to see where the throw is coming, and then back up either base.

CATCHER: Cover home plate.

FIRST BASEMAN: Be the cutoff man.

SECOND BASEMAN: Become relay man.

THIRD BASEMAN: Cover 3B.

SHORTSTOP: Be trailer relay man, then return and cover 2B.

LEFT FIELDER: Move into area behind 3B.

RIGHT FIELDER AND CENTER FIELDER: Go after ball.

DEFENSIVE ASSIGNMENTS

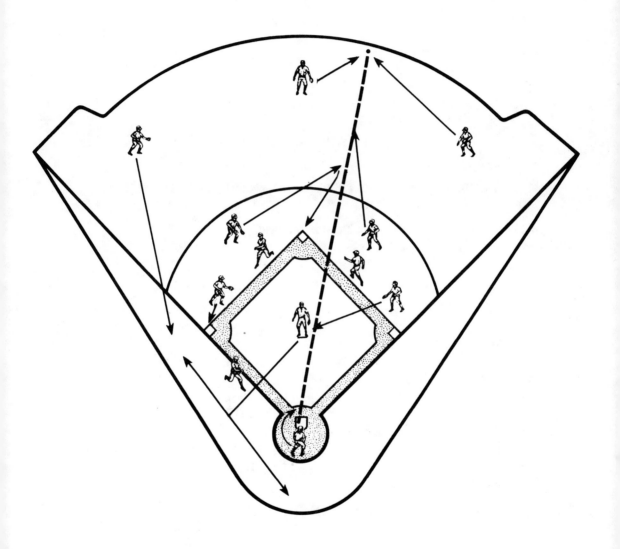

SITUATION 21

SITUATION 22

DOUBLE, POSSIBLE TRIPLE, DOWN RIGHT-FIELD LINE

No one on base.

PITCHER: Back up 3B.

CATCHER: Protect home-plate area.

FIRST BASEMAN: Backup or safety-valve man.

SECOND BASEMAN: Become first relay man.

SHORTSTOP: To 2B and then to cutoff position for throw to 3B.

THIRD BASEMAN: Cover 3B.

LEFT FIELDER: Move into an area behind 3B.

CENTER FIELDER: Back up right fielder.

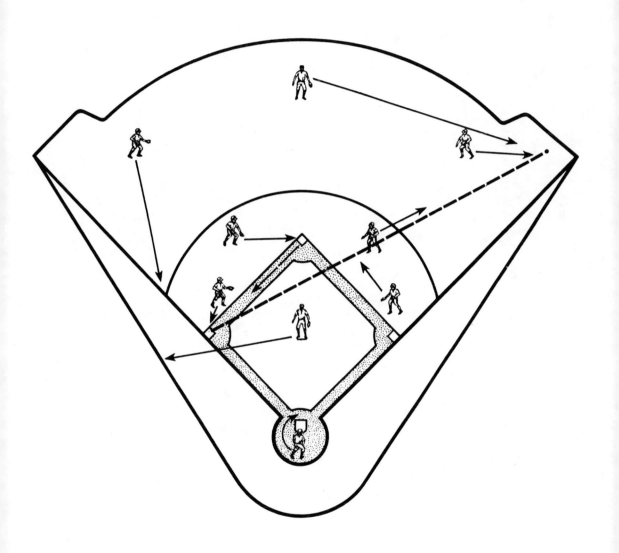

SITUATION 22

SITUATION 23

DOUBLE, POSSIBLE TRIPLE, DOWN RIGHT-FIELD LINE

Man on 1B.

PITCHER: Go halfway between 3B and home to see where throw is going.

CATCHER: Cover home plate.

FIRST BASEMAN: Trail second baseman—remain about 30 feet back.

SECOND BASEMAN: Relay man. Go to a spot in right field along foul line in line with right fielder and home.

SHORTSTOP: Cover 2B, then to cutoff position for throw to 3B.

THIRD BASEMAN: Cover 3B.

LEFT FIELDER: Move in toward 3B.

CENTER FIELDER: Back up right fielder.

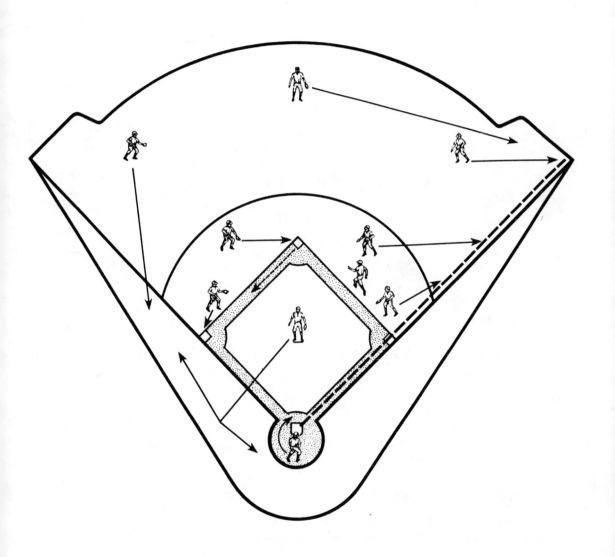

SITUATION 23

POP-FLY SITUATION 1

A FOUL FLY IS HIT BEHIND THE PLATE

Runners on 1B and 3B*
Less than two out.

PITCHER: Cover home plate.

CATCHER: Catch pop-up and throw to cutoff man.

FIRST BASEMAN: Help on pop-up.

SECOND BASEMAN: Become cutoff man behind the pitcher's mound.

THIRD BASEMAN: Cover 3B.

SHORTSTOP: Cover 2B.

LEFT FIELDER: Come in to help back up shortstop and 3B area.

CENTER FIELDER: Back up 2B.

RIGHT FIELDER: Cover 1B.

* Both runners tag up and runner on 1B breaks for 2B. If there is no cutoff man, the runner on 3B will score easily when the catcher makes his throw to 2B.

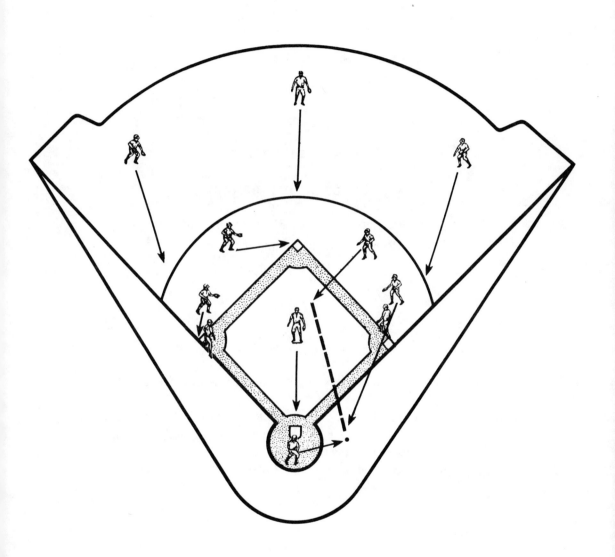

POP-FLY SITUATION 1

POP-FLY SITUATION 2

A POP FLY IS HIT BEHIND 1B

Runners on 1B and 3B, and none out
Both runners tag up and the runner
on 1B breaks for 2B.

PITCHER: Cover 1B.

CATCHER: Cover home plate.

FIRST BASEMAN: Go for pop-up.

SECOND BASEMAN: Also go after the pop-up; call play if 1B or outfield makes catch.

SHORTSTOP: Cover 2B.

THIRD BASEMAN: Cover 3B.

LEFT FIELDER: Move into an area behind 3B for backup man.

CENTER FIELDER: Back up 2B.

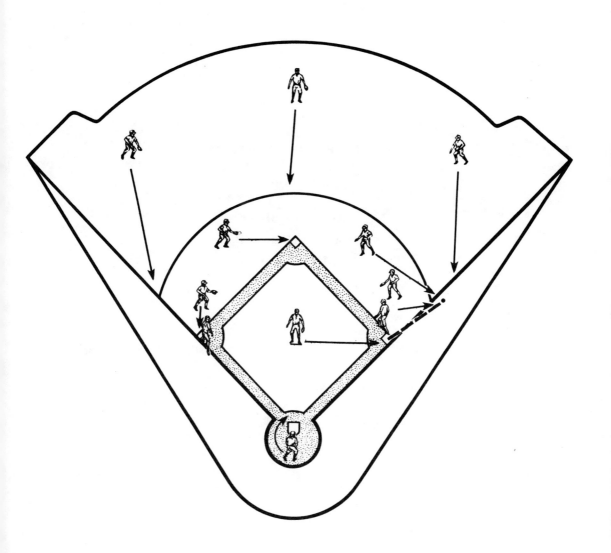

POP-FLY SITUATION 2

WILD PITCHES AND PASSED BALLS

SITUATION 1

Runner on 3B, or
Runners on 1B and 3B, or
On 1B, 2B and 3B.

PITCHER: Cover home plate.

CATCHER: Retrieve the ball.

FIRST BASEMAN: Back up the plate.

SECOND BASEMAN: Cover 2B.

SHORTSTOP: Cover 3B.

THIRD BASEMAN: Back up plate at the mound.

All outfielders move toward the infield area to help where needed.

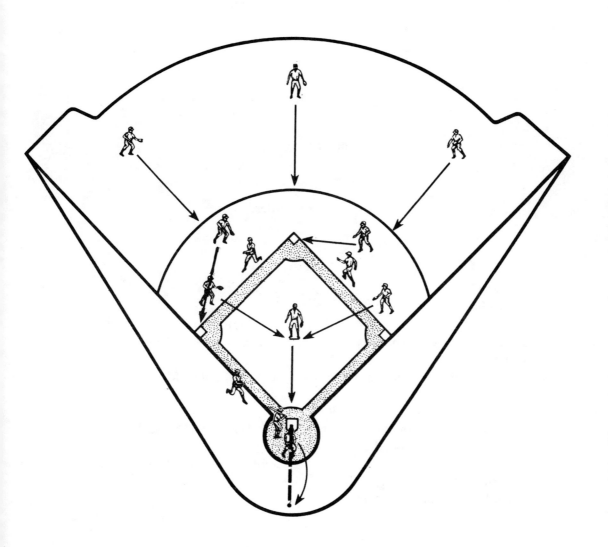

WILD PITCHES AND PASSED BALLS

SITUATION 1

BUNT SITUATION 1

Runner on 1B,

Bunt in order.

PITCHER: Break toward plate after delivering the ball.

CATCHER: Field all bunts possible; call the play; cover 3B when third baseman fields the bunt in close to home plate.

FIRST BASEMAN: Cover the area between 1B and the mound.

SECOND BASEMAN: Cover 1B . . . cheat by shortening position.

SHORTSTOP: Cover 2B.

THIRD BASEMAN: Cover the area between 3B and the mound.

LEFT FIELDER: Move in toward 2B area.

CENTER FIELDER: Back up 2B.

RIGHT FIELDER: Back up 1B.

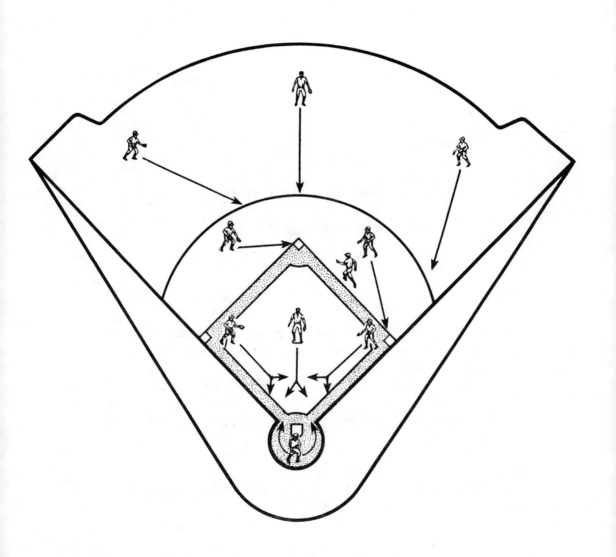

BUNT SITUATION 1

BUNT SITUATION 2

REGULAR BUNT PLAY

With runners on 1B and 2B,
Bunt situation in order.

PITCHER: Break toward 3B line upon delivering the ball, and either make necessary play or call for third baseman to make play.

CATCHER: Field bunts in front of plate; *call the play*.

FIRST BASEMAN: Be responsible for all balls in the area between 1B and a direct line from the mound to home.

SECOND BASEMAN: Cover 1B.

SHORTSTOP: Hold runner close to bag before pitch; cover 2B.

THIRD BASEMAN: Take position on the edge of the grass; be prepared to make play as called by pitcher.

LEFT FIELDER: Back up 3B.

CENTER FIELDER: Back up 2B.

RIGHT FIELDER: Back up 1B.

First objective is to retire the runner at 3B, but one runner *must* be retired.

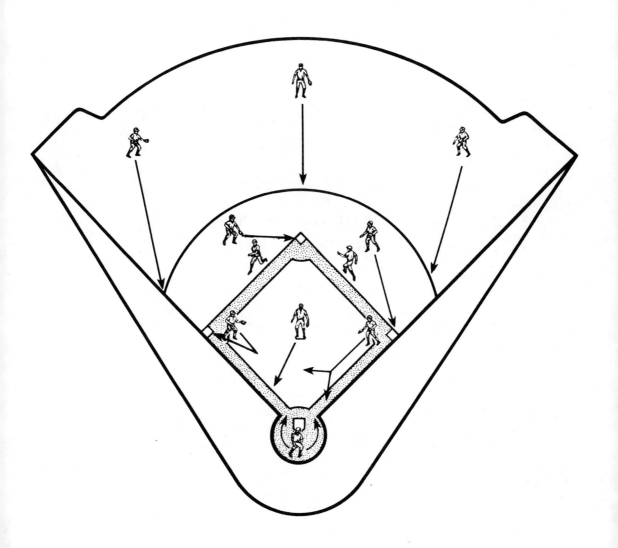

BUNT SITUATION 2

BUNT SITUATION 3

3B CHARGE PLAY

Runners on 1B and 2B,
Bunt situation in order.

PITCHER: Cover 1B side.

CATCHER: Field bunts in front of plate or *call the play*.

FIRST BASEMAN: Cover 1B.

SECOND BASEMAN: Cover 2B.

SHORTSTOP: Bluff runner back to 2B then race to cover 3B.

THIRD BASEMAN: Charge toward the plate.

OUTFIELDERS: Move in toward infield area on *all* bunt situations.

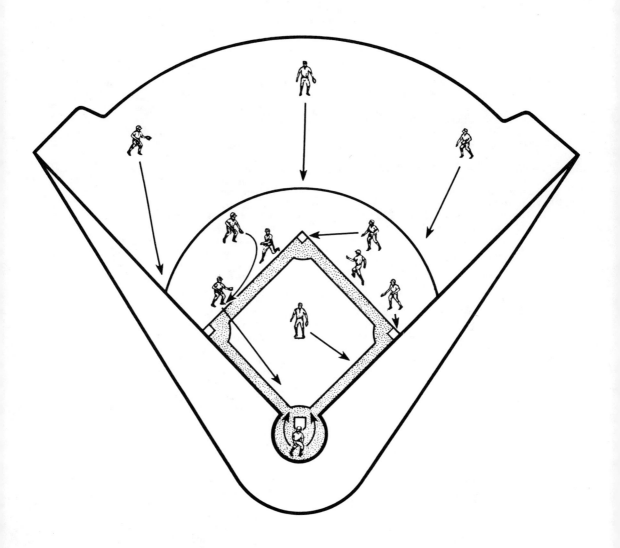

BUNT SITUATION 3

INDEX

INDEX

INDEX

INDEX